SAVING THE NATIVE SON:

EMPOWERMENT STRATEGIES

FOR YOUNG BLACK MALES

by

Courtland C. Lee
University of Virginia

ERIC Counseling and Student Services Clearinghouse
School of Education
University of North Carolina at Greensboro
Greensboro, North Carolina 27412-5001
1-800-414-9769

DEDICATION

To the memory of Alfred B. Pasteur, Ph.D.,
my mentor and my friend.

ERIC/CASS Publications
School of Education
University of North Carolina at Greensboro
Greensboro, NC 27412
1-800-414-9769

ISBN 1-56109-063-8

This publication was funded by the U.S. Department of
Education, Office of Educational Research and Improvement,
Contract No. RR93002004. Opinions expressed in this
publication do not necessarily reflect the positions of the
U.S. Department of Education, OERI, or ERIC/CASS.

INTRODUCTION

If past performance is a good predictor of the future, this monograph will be extremely well received and used by a wide variety of persons—educators, counselors, psychologists, and community specialists as well as concerned parents. The first volume published in 1992 responded to a universal need for a better understanding of young Black males. Unlike many books on young Black males, Dr. Lee provided cogent insights into young Black male development and behavior, but admirably also offered practical and compelling strategies and interventions for empowering young Black males so they might better cope with the myriad challenges they must face on the road to achieving manhood.

Readers who, to their great satisfaction, found both inspiration and practical help in *Empowering Young Black Males* will be pleased with the expanded coverage of the previous topics and especially the addition of three new chapters focused on Black parenting, how other racial or ethnic persons may be helpful, and innovative ideas on self help for young Black males. Prospective new readers, be they mental health professionals or interested parents and/or community members, will appreciate Dr. Lee's clear and informative writing and his attention to offering viable and effective strategies for contributing to the empowerment of young Black males.

For those whose learning style benefits from video experiences, an excellent video tape is available featuring an interaction between Dr. Lee and Ms. Cheryl Holcomb, a former school counselor who interacts on key issues and topics relating to young Black males. A noteworthy part of the tape is a series of role playing demonstrations by Dr. Lee as to how to respond to a number of situations involving young Black male decision making.

In short, this is a book that can be of great help to anyone who is motivated to learn more about young Black males and how he/she can contribute to their empowerment. The special appeal of this book is that it both enhances knowledge and understanding, but also provides practical strategies and interventions that can make a difference. We all are indebted to Dr. Lee for his providing us with a much needed and very worthwhile publication.

Garry R. Walz
Director and Editor-in-Chief

ABOUT THE AUTHOR

Courtland C. Lee is a Professor of Counselor Education at the University of Virginia. His research specialties include multicultural counseling and adolescent development. He is the editor of two books on multicultural counseling. In addition, he has published numerous articles and book chapters on adolescent development and counseling across cultures.

Dr. Lee is the editor of the *Journal of African American Men* and currently serves on the advisory board of the *International Journal for the Advancement of Counselling*. He is also the former editor of the *Journal of Multicultural Counseling and Development*. His activities in national and international professional organizations include service as past president of the *Association for Multicultural Counseling and Development*, a division of the *American Counseling Association*, membership in the Executive Council of the *International Round Table for the Advancement of Counselling*, serving as that organization's representative to the United Nations, and membership in the *British Association for Counselling*.

A former teacher and school counselor, Dr. Lee has served as a psychoeducational consultant on Black male issues to numerous educational institutions both in the United States and abroad.

ACKNOWLEDGMENTS

I am indebted to a number of individuals for their assistance with the development of *Saving the Native Son: Empowerment Strategies for Young Black Males.* First, and foremost are the professional counselors and other educators, both in the United States and abroad, who expressed interest in my first book and who attended my workshops and seminars on empowering young Black males. I am greatly impressed with their dedication and commitment to the cause of Black male youth. These individuals have taken my empowerment modules back to their jobs and implemented them in creative ways. Many of their ideas for improving the empowerment modules are presented in this book. I am grateful for their efforts.

I am most appreciative to Dr. Garry R. Walz, Director of ERIC/CASS for his encouragement, support and ideas during the writing of this book and Dr. Jeanne C. Bleuer, Associate Director, for her overall interest and enthusiasm.

A word of thanks must go to Professor Nathan Deen, Erika Stern, and Peter de Weerdt of the Department of Counselling Studies at the University of Utrecht in The Netherlands for their interest in my work on Black male empowerment. I appreciate their efforts in promoting my first book among Dutch educational professionals.

Likewise, I must thank Dr. Diana Shumkler formerly of the Psychology Department at the University of the Witwatersrand in Johannesburg, South Africa for providing me the opportunity to share my empowerment ideas in that country. Concerned about the future of her country, she made it possible for me to travel to South Africa to share my work.

My most heartfelt appreciation to Dr. Richard Majors, President Emeritus of The National Council of African

American Men, Inc., and an eminent scholar of Black male development in his own right, for his enthusiastic promotion of my first book. He has spoken highly of my empowerment work throughout the country and for that I am most grateful.

Finally, I am deeply grateful to my wife, Antoinette, for her love and support. As with the development of the first book, I greatly appreciate having the benefit of her experiences and insights.

PREFACE *

"Mr. Max, a guy gets tired of being told what he can do and can't do. You get a little job here and a little job there. You shine shoes, sweep streets; anything....You don't make enough to live on. You don't know when you going to get fired. Pretty soon you get so you can't hope for nothing. You just keep moving all the time, doing what other folks say. You ain't a man no more. You just work day in and day out so the world can roll on and other people can live.

Richard Wright, *Native Son*

The excerpt above comes from the novel *Native Son,* the literary masterpiece by the African American author, Richard Wright. The book tells the story of the systematic psychological and social destruction of a young Black man by a racist sociopolitical system. *Native Son* captures the powerful emotions, suffering, frustrations, and yearnings that generally typified growing up Black and male in 1940s America.

When considered from a current psychoeducational perspective, Wright's story of Bigger Thomas, the *"native son,"* still resonates with truth and power. Black males in contemporary American society face major challenges to their psychological and social development. Social and economic indicators of Black male development in the United States provide a profile of individuals whose quality of life is in serious jeopardy. From an early age, it has become increasingly apparent that Black males are confronted with a series of obstacles in their attempts to attain academic, career, and personal-social success.

Achieving manhood has historically been a complex and challenging task for the Black male in America. Therefore,

* Please note that the terms Black and African American are used interchangeably throughout the book. Both terms reflect thinking about appropriate ethnic identification for Americans who trace their roots to Africa.

Black manhood must be carefully fostered from an early age by major socializing agents and institutions. Parents and the family represent the most important socializing agents and institutions for young males. However, the school and community can also play significant roles as socializing institutions for young Black males.

In 1992, *Empowering Young Black Males* addressed the issues and challenges facing this group of young Americans. The book provided school counselors and related professionals with important information needed to confront the crisis of the Black male. The book focused on how professional school counselors could promote Black male educational empowerment in the school setting. This book has proven to be highly successful, having enjoyed widespread use by practicing school counselors. It has also been adopted by professionals in a variety of community service and social welfare institutions. In addition, the book has been used in a number of classes and workshops and is frequently quoted and cited. The concepts presented in the book have also found relevancy in educational and social empowerment work with ethnic minority male youth in The Netherlands and South Africa.

The success of *Empowering Young Black Males has* spawned the development of this book, *Saving the Native Son: Empowerment Strategies for Young Black Males,* which is developed in the spirit and context of its predecessor. *Saving the Native Son* builds on the strategies and techniques offered in *Empowering Young Black Males.* This new book provides counselors and related mental-health professionals, community leaders, and parents with important information about the development of young Black males that has emerged since the publication of *Empowering Young Black Males.* This latest book, which features three new chapters, updates empowerment modules for promoting the academic and social development of Black male youth. It also suggests ways to actively involve both teachers and the inherent strengths of Black communities in this important process.

Chapter 1 sets the stage for the book by offering an overview and interpretation of current statistical data on Black male development. Chapter 2 examines the early psychosocial development of Black males along with the historical and environmental impediments to childhood and adolescent Black male development. Chapter 3 discusses African/African-American culture and its role in the development of Black male youth. Chapter 4 profiles an educational empowerment program for promoting optimal academic achievement and positive social behavior among Black males at the elementary school level. An empowerment intervention for promoting manhood among Black males in Grades 7 through 12 is presented in Chapter 5. In Chapter 6, a guide for getting men from Black communities involved in educational empowerment efforts with young boys is offered. Chapter 7 focuses on educational advocacy for Black male youth. It provides direction for counselor consultations to help teachers and other educators understand the dynamics of Black male development. A curriculum for the professional development of school personnel in understanding Black males and in promoting their academic success is also presented. Chapter 8 is one of the three new chapters. It describes a workshop to help Black parents, particularly single Black mothers, promote the academic and social development of their sons. The second of the new chapters is Chapter 9, which explains how individuals from other racial or ethnic groups, in particular White men, can help empower Black male youth. Chapter 10 is the third new chapter and it explores a principle of self-help for Black male youth. Chapter 11 ends the book with a call to action for professional counselors that presents a comprehensive plan for the empowerment of young black males.

This book is designed as an action manual for all those concerned about promoting the development of the next generation of African American men. The concepts and programs presented here are designed to guide initiatives for promoting the academic, career, and personal-social empowerment of young Black males. It is hoped that the awareness and knowledge gained, as well as the skills developed, from this book will help concerned individuals to become a part of the solution, rather than a part of the problem.

CONTENTS

"African-American males have historically been at risk since being brought as human chattel to what is now the United States. They were at risk from the time of their recorded presence in 1619, and unfortunately are still in a vulnerable state in 1990, three hundred and seventy-one years later."

The Task Force to Address The Decline of Enrollment and Graduation of the Black Male from Institutions of Higher Education, January, 1990

"Bigger, are there many Negro boys like you?"
"I reckon so. All of 'em I know ain't got nothing and ain't going nowhere."

Richard Wright, Native Son, 1940

CHAPTER ONE

THE BLACK MALE IN CONTEMPORARY SOCIETY: SOCIAL AND EDUCATIONAL CHALLENGES

Black males in contemporary society face many challenges that shape their physical, psychological, and social development. Evidence from both popular and social science literature over the last decade suggest that Black men in the United States constitute a population at risk (Cordes, 1985; Dent, 1989; Gibbs, 1988; Johnson & Watson, 1990; Jones, 1986; Long & Farr, 1991; McCall, 1994; Monroe, 1987; Parham & McDavis, 1987; Randolph, 1990; Salholz, 1990; Weathers, 1993; Wright, 1992). Most social and economic indicators for Black men depict individuals whose development and quality of life are in serious jeopardy. In 1990, for example, the National Urban League released a report on the status of the African American male (Johnson & Watson, 1990). This report offered a disturbing portrait of Black male life. It stated that Black males have a shorter life span than any other population group in America, due to a disproportionate vulnerability to disease and homicide. In every age group, Black men are significantly more likely to be victims of violent crime than are White men or women of either race. Among youths ages 14 to 17, the Black male victimization rate is 65.9 per 100,000 in the population; the White male rate is 8.5 (U.S. Bureau of Justice Statistics 1986).

The Urban League report also points out that structural changes in the labor market and discriminatory hiring practices create wide gaps between the earnings of Black and White men, and a disproportionate number of Black men living in poverty. Significantly, unemployment figures for African American males are 2.3 times higher than for White males and indicate that in 1988, less than one third of African American males between the ages of 16 and 19 were employed (Holister, 1989; United States Bureau of the Census, 1990).

Additionally, the report states that an internalized negative self-image on the part of many Black males and the negative attitudes of authority figures toward them along with increased violence and drug abuse results in a disproportionate involvement of Black males with the criminal justice system. In 1989, for example, there were 609,690 young African American men involved in the U.S. justice system. This figure represents 23% of African American men between the ages of 20 and 29. With only 436,000 African American males enrolled in higher education, the figure representing those African American males involved in the criminal justice system is 39.8% higher than those enrolled in higher education (Mauer, 1990).

In addition to statistics such as these, Black males encounter negative stereotypes about their very manhood. These stereotypes include notions of social castration, insecurity in their male identity, and a negative self-concept. Significantly, most of these stereotypes have stemmed from a failure to understand masculinity in an African American social and cultural context (Staples, 1978).

From birth to death, it is apparent that Black males in America face a series of challenges to optimal development. These challenges take their toll at every age, but at every stage of life the toll is very high and the effect is cumulative (McGhee, 1984). Collectively, Black males are often powerless and generally find themselves marginalized in contemporary society.

The Educational Challenges of Young Black Males

The central challenge facing young Black males in contemporary society is an inadequate education. (Green & Wright, 1991; Johnson & Watson, 1990; Narine, 1992; Reed, 1988; Wright, 1992) Black males encounter formidable challenges to their educational development and many of them experience a serious stifling of achievement, aspiration and pride in school systems throughout the country.

A Profile in Failure

Data on the educational attainment of Black male youth from a variety of sources (Committee on Education and Labor, 1990; House of Representatives, 1989, Jones, 1986; Johnson & Watson, 1990; Joint Economic Committee, 1991; Narine, 1992; National Black Child Development Institute, 1990; Reed, 1988) present a profile of widespread failure. For example:

- Black males are far more likely than other ethnic/ gender groups to be placed in general education and vocational high school curricular tracks than in an academic track.
- Black males are three times more likely to be placed in classes for the educable mentally retarded and for students with learning disabilities than in gifted and talented classes.
- Black males drop out or are pushed out of school systems at higher rates than other ethnic/gender groups.
- Black males are suspended from school more frequently and for longer periods of time than other ethnic/ gender groups.
- Black males complete high school at significantly lower rates than other ethnic/gender groups.

- Between 1976 and 1986, despite increases in overall minority enrollment, including Black female enrollment, college enrollment rates of Black males 18-24 declined from 35% to 28%.

What is evident from this profile is that Black males tend to experience massive alienation from America's schools. Significantly, a recent report prepared by a committee to study the status of the Black male in the New Orleans Public Schools graphically underscores these data. Though Black males represented 43% of the public school population in that city during the 1986-87 academic year, they accounted for 58% of the non-promotions, 65% of the suspensions, 80% of the expulsions, and 45% of the dropouts (Committee to Study the Status of the Black Male in the New Orleans Public Schools, 1988).

This report from the New Orleans Public Schools is by no means an anomaly. Indications of massive academic failure on the part of Black males can be found in school systems across the country. Such failure often begins as early as the third grade, with many Black males either dropping out or being pushed out of school for behavioral problems by the seventh grade.

Such data and reports are compounded by the fact that Black males are frequently the victims of negative attitudes and lowered expectations from teachers, counselors, and administrators. Educators may expect to encounter academic and social problems from Black males, which often leads to a self-fulfilling prophecy (Washington & Lee, 1982). As recipients of lowered expectations from teachers, counselors, and administrators, Black males experience alienation in school, making failure an all too common part of their educational experience.

It is apparent that Black males face major academic and social hurdles. While many Black males achieve significant educational success, many others experience prohibitive challenges, often becoming frustrated, losing hope, and ultimately dropping out or being pushed out of school. The consequences of this are significant limitations on socioeconomic mobility, ultimately leading to high rates of unemployment, crime, and incarceration for growing numbers of young Black men.

African-Centered Academies for Black Male Youth: A Radical Concept?

Importantly, efforts are under way to promote the educational development of young Black males. One effort, for example, is the establishment of separate public schools or classes for Black male youth where the emphasis is on raising self-respect, promoting racial and cultural pride, and overcoming obstacles to educational success (Freiberg, 1991; Narine, 1992). Narine (1992) presents a comprehensive analysis of the educational policy, that is being adopted by or considered in many public school systems to separate Black male youth from the general school population. She describes separate educational programs for Black male youth established in the Detroit and Milwaukee public school systems. In both programs, Black male youth are separated into single-gender, single-race classes or "academies" that are staffed by adult Black male faculty. The curriculum in these programs is multicultural in nature with an African American or *"Afrocentric"* focus. It is geared to foster motivation for learning and to provide the youth with a positive sense of self as African/African-American people. Additionally, with a Black male faculty, these educational initiatives seek to provide students with significant role models and mentors.

As a result of the efforts in Detroit and Milwaukee, school systems throughout the country have considered opening schools or providing classes exclusively for Black male youth. These all-male institutions have sparked fierce debate (Biggs,

1992; Collison, 1991; Greathouse & Sparling, 1993; Holland, 1987; Kantrowitz, 1990; Whitaker, 1991). In 1990, the NAACP Legal Defense and Educational Fund summarized the major objections to separate schools for young Black males: it is feared that the success of such schools will undermine long-standing efforts to desegregate American schools; these school will deny the benefits of positive male influences and multicultural curriculum to Black female youth; there is no evidence that race or gender segregated schools will be educationally or developmentally superior; such schools serve to blame the victim, i.e. they implicitly place the blame for negative educational experiences on Black male youth; and there are significant questions and concerns about how such schools can co-exist with federal civil rights statutes that prohibit recipients of federal funds from segregating or treating students differently on the basis of race or gender.

While there is, as of yet, no conclusive evidence that separate schools for young Black males significantly improve academic performance or promote positive self-concept, there are encouraging signs that these efforts have the potential to empower male youth in a nontraditional and innovative fashion (Black Issues in Higher Education, 1994). As these schools continue to develop, educators are realizing the importance of using whatever means within their power to promote school success among young Black males. The distressing figures related to Black male educational attainment appear to demand no less of an effort.

Empowering Young Black Males:
Implications for Educators and
Community Leaders

The book also explores important concepts that educators and others must understand and appreciate if they are to be effective agents of empowerment for Black male youth. These concepts focus on appreciating male development in childhood and adolescence from an African American cultural perspective.

At a time when rapidly changing technology requires a skilled and well-educated workforce, Black males are losing ground at a perilous rate. This troubling situation calls for aggressive action by educators and other concerned individuals. They are faced with the challenge of insuring that young Black males are provided educational opportunities that will maximize their potential. Concerted efforts are needed to develop comprehensive approaches for facilitating the academic, career, and personal-social development of young Black males. Such approaches should reflect the needs and realities of Black male students. The single-sex, single-race public school concept discussed above certainly represents such an approach. The major portion of this book examines another approach. It offers specific strategies considered necessary for empowering young Black males for optimal educational achievement and social success. Empowerment is a developmental process by which people who are powerless or marginalized become aware of the power dynamics at work in their lives. They develop the skills and capacity for gaining a degree of control over their lives, which they then exercise without infringing upon the rights of others. All this coincides with the general empowerment of others in their community (Hawley-McWhirter, 1994).

The book also explores important concepts that educators and others must understand and appreciate if they are to be effective agents of empowerment for Black male youth. These concepts focus on appreciating male development in childhood and adolescence from an African American cultural perspective.

Conclusion

Education is power. It is a lifelong process of developing the knowledge and skills to be all that one can be. Black people have always placed a great value on education. Indeed, Blacks' social and economic progress in this country has been in direct proportion to the educational opportunities available to them.

Black males in contemporary American society, however, face formidable challenges to their educational development. Those concerned with Black male youth must stand ready to address the frustration, underachievement, and ultimate failure that comprise the educational reality for scores of Black male youth.

REFERENCES

Biggs, S.A. (1992). The plight of Black males in American schools: Separation may not be the answer. *The Negro Educational Review, 43*, 11-16.

Black Issues in Higher Education (1994, February 24). *Detroit's African-centered academies disarm skeptics, empower boys*, p. 18-21.

Collison, M. (1991). Black male schools? Yes. *Black Enterprise*, p. 41.

Committee to Study the Status of the Black Male in the New Orleans Public Schools. (1988). *Educating Black male youth: A moral and civic imperative. An introspective look at Black male students in the New Orleans Public Schools*. New Orleans, LA: Orleans Parish School Board.

Cordes, C. (1985, January). At risk in America: Black males face high odds in a hostile society. *APA Monitor,* pp. 9, 10, 11, 27

Dent, D. (1989, November). Readin', ritin' and rage: How schools are destroying black boys. *Essence,* pp. 54-59, 114-116.

Freiberg, P. (1991, May). Separate classes for Black males? *APA Monitor,* pp. 1, 47.

Gary, L.W. (Ed.). (1981). *Black men.* Beverly Hills, CA: Sage Publications.

Gibbs, J. T. (1984). Black adolescents and youth: An endangered species. *American Journal of Orthopsychiatry, 54,* 6-21.

Gibbs, J. T. (Ed.). (1988). *Young, Black, and male in America: An endangered species.* New York: Auburn House.

Greathouse, B. & Sparling, S. (1993). African American male-only schools: Is that the solution? *Childhood Education, 69,* 131-132.

Green, R. L. & Wright, D. L. (1991, March). African American males: A demographic study and analysis. Paper presented at the National Workshop of the W.K. Kellog Foundation, Sacramento, CA.

Hawley-McWhirter, E. (1994). *Empowerment in counseling.* Alexandria, VA: American Counseling Association.

Holister, R. G. (1989). *Youth employment and training programs.* Washington, DC: National Academy Press.

Holland, S. (1987, March). A radical approach to educating young Black males. *Education Week,* pp.1-2.

House of Representatives. (1989). *Barriers and opportunities for America's young Black men. Hearing before the select committee on children, youth, and families.* Washington, DC: U.S. Government Printing Office.

House of Representatives. (1990). *Hearing on the Office of Educational Research and Improvement. Hearing before the subcommittee on select education of the committee on education and labor.* Washington, DC: U.S. Government Printing Office.

Johnson, J. M. & Watson, B. C. (Eds.). (1990). *Stony the road they trod: The African American male.* Washington, D.C.: National Urban League, Inc.

Jones, K. M. (1986). Black male in jeopardy. *Crisis, 93,* 16-21, 44-45.

Kantrowitz, B. (1990, October). Can the boys be saved? *Newsweek, 116,* p.67.

Leavy, W. (1983, August). Is the Black male an endangered species? *Ebony.* pp. 40-49.

Mauer, M. (1990). *Young Black men and the criminal justice system: A growing national problem.* Washington, DC: The Sentencing Project.

NAACP Legal Defense and Educational Fund. (1990). *Statement on proposals for separate schools for African American male pupils.* New York: Author

McCall, N. (1994). *Makes me wanna holler: A young Black man in America.* New York: Random House.

McGhee, J. D. (1984) *Running the gauntlet: Black men in America.* New York: National Urban League.

Monroe, S. (1987, March). Brothers. *Newsweek, 109,* pp. 54-66.

Narine, M. L. (1992). *Single-sex, single race public schools: A solution to the problems plaguing the Black community?* Washington, DC: U.S. Department of Education.

National Black Child Development Institute. (1990). *The status of African American children: Twentieth Anniversary Report 1970-1990.* Washington, DC: National Black Child Development Institute.

Parham, T. & McDavis, R. (1987). Black men, an endangered species: Who's really pulling the trigger? *Journal of Counseling and Development, 66,* 24-27.

Randolph, (1990, August). What can we do about the most explosive problem in black America - the widening gap between women who are making it and men who aren't. *Ebony,* p. 52.

Reed, R. J. (1988). Education and achievement of young Black males. In J. T. Gibbs (Ed.) *Young, Black, and male in America: An endangered species,* pp.37-96. New York: Auburn House.

Salholz, E. (1990, December). Short lives, bloody deaths: Black murder rates soar. *Newsweek, 116,* p. 116.

United States Bureau of the Census. (1990). *Statistical abstracts of the United States: 1989.* Washington, DC: U.S. Government Printing Office.

U.S. Department of Justice, Bureau of Justice Statistics. (1986). *Correctional population in the United States - 1986.* Washington, D.C.

Washington, V., & Lee, C. C. (1982). Teaching and counseling Black males in grades K to 8. *Journal of the National Association of Black Social Workers, 13,* 25-29.

Weathers, D. (1993, December). Stop the guns. *Essence.,* pp. 70-71, 132-137.

Whitaker, C. (1991, March). Do Black males need special schools? *Ebony, pp.* 17-22.

Wright, W. (1992). The endangered Black male child. *Educational Leadership, 49*, 14-16.

CHAPTER TWO

THE PSYCHOSOCIAL DEVELOPMENT OF YOUNG BLACK MALES: ISSUES AND IMPEDIMENTS

Introduction

Successful implementation of empowerment initiatives for young Black males must be predicated on an understanding of the dynamics associated with childhood and adolescent psychosocial development from a Black male perspective. This chapter provides an overview of important historical and social issues that must be considered in the psychosocial development of young Black males.

Key Developmental Issues of Childhood and Adolescence

Theorists and researchers have suggested that major aspects of human development unfold in a series of life stages which are influenced by both heredity and environment (Erikson, 1950; Havighurst, 1972; Kohlberg, 1966; Piaget, 1970). As individuals progress through the life stages, they must master a series of developmental tasks. Mastery of tasks at one stage of life influences success with those in succeeding stages. Conversely, failure to master developmental tasks at one stage can impede success in later stages.

Erikson (1950), for example, succinctly conceptualized the developmental stages and tasks of childhood and adolescence. Childhood is the period in life when an individual must develop a sense of trust, autonomy, initiative, and industry. These dimensions can be seen in such things as a child learning to relate emotionally to parents and siblings, learning to walk and talk, developing a self-concept, and learning to read and write.

Adolescence follows. This is the period when an individual begins the important life transition from childhood to adulthood. It is during this span of time that a child should develop a sense of identity that is observable in events such as learning gender appropriate social roles and behaviors, achieving emotional independence from significant adults, and setting educational and career goals.

It is important to note that for Black males in America, successfully completing these early developmental stages and tasks has often been problematic due to a complex set of historical and social factors. In many instances, these factors interact in such a manner that Black males are forced to deal with additional developmental tasks in their psychosocial development. Crawley and Freeman (1993) have described an additional series of developmental tasks and socialization issues that confront Black males in childhood and adolescence. These tasks and issues are most directly influenced by race, ethnicity, and culture and represent Crawley and Freeman's expansion on traditional psychosocial theoretical concepts. This expanded list is the result of their analysis of the life themes and views of both younger and older Black males. According to Crawley and Freeman's analysis, in addition to the universal psychosocial developmental tasks and issues everyone must face, historical and social dynamics force Black males to complete added steps during childhood and adolescence:

CHILDHOOD
- recognition of self and others based on color
- incorporate racial labels into evolving self-concept
- recognize, identify and label social inconsistencies, e.g. racism, discrimination, prejudice
- recognize and develop skills for negotiating multi-racial environments and bicultural experiences, each containing mixed and contradictory messages
- forge an appropriate and healthy identity in the face of racism, discrimination, prejudice
- fine-tune sensing and judging skills to screen out or transform negative racial/color images and messages

ADOLESCENCE
- refine healthy identity which transforms and/or transcends societal messages of inferiority, pathology, and deviance based on color, race and/or culture
- strengthen skills for negotiating bicultural and multicultural environments

Black males are often prevented from mastering both these crucial universal and race-specific developmental tasks in childhood and adolescence. In turn, this lack of mastery retards their academic, career, and social success in the later stages of life.

Impediments to the Psychosocial Development of Black Males

From an historical perspective, manhood has not been a birthright for Black males (Hernton, 1965; Lee, 1990; Staples, 1978). They have not generally been granted traditional masculine privilege or power in the United States. Social, cultural, and economic forces throughout American history have combined to keep Black males from assuming accepted masculine roles (Staples, 1983; Wilkinson & Taylor, 1977). The White male, from boyhood, is generally socialized with a masculine sensibility comprised of an awareness that power and control are his birthright. He naturally assumes the primary means of insuring personal respect, financial security, and success (Goldberg, 1976; Pleck & Sawyer, 1974) The Black male, on the other hand, has often been denied such possibilities of manhood. This denial anchors dynamics of oppression and racism that have pervaded the Black experience in America (Grier & Cobbs, 1968; Thomas & Sillen, 1972). Beginning with slavery, the Black male has been an object of fear (Grier & Cobbs, 1968; Hilliard, 1985; Staples, 1978). The Black man, and his implied physical prowess and leadership ability, has been perceived as representing the greatest threat to the social order. Therefore, the power structure within American society has insured that Black males have had limited access to the traditional sex-role values and behaviors associated with power, control, status, and achievement. Throughout American history, the power structure has initiated various social and economic actions that have resulted in the subordination of the Black male and the cancellation of his masculine advantage in the larger society (Staples, 1978; Taylor, 1977). In many cases, the inability to attain masculine roles has kept Black men from realizing even the most basic aspects of masculine privilege and power, namely life-sustaining employment and the ability to support a family (Staples, 1978).

The persistence of barriers to the achievement and expression of manhood has generally resulted in significant social disadvantages for Black males. Such disadvantages have contributed to the failure of Black males, in many instances, to master crucial developmental tasks in childhood and adolescence. In a society that historically has not acknowledged manhood as a birthrighfor Black males, achieving optimal psychosocial development has been difficult for Black male youth.

It is not uncommon to find environmental forces converging to cripple the psychosocial development of scores of Black males in contemporary society (Chestang, 1980; Madhubuti, 1990; Staples, 1987). Blacks are often confronted with extreme environmental stress during the crucial early years of life (Hilliard, 1985; Myers & King, 1980). This stress is manifested in home, community, and school experiences. For example, a majority of Black male youth, particularly in urban areas, are born in homes and communities characterized by traditions of poverty, crime, unemployment, inequitable educational opportunities, and a perceived sense of social and cultural alienation among many men. Young boys nurtured in such environments may experience difficulty in developing the basic trust, sense of autonomy, initiative, and industry which characterize the developmental tasks of the childhood years. Additionally, they may experience trouble forming a basic identity as a Black male and developing the skills for negotiating multiracial environments, which are requisite developmental tasks in the race-specific developmental paradigm conceptualized by Crawley and Freeman (1993).

Successful completion of developmental tasks can be further hampered by ineffective teaching strategies, as well as educators' predetermined negative views of Black males and their learning potential (Washington & Lee, 1982). Rather than developing a sense of industry that comes with mastering fundamental skills in reading, writing, and computing during the all-important elementary school years, many young Black male students experience a sense of frustration with education, thus laying the groundwork for future academic and social failure.

It is not unusual, therefore, for Black males to reach adolescence with a basic mistrust of their environment, doubts about their abilities, and confusion about their place in the social structure. This makes developing an identity during the crucial boyhood-to-manhood transition of the adolescent years extremely problematic. Compounding this problem is the social reality that Black male youth may have to form identities with either minimal or no positive adult male role modeling. Significantly, identity-formation during adolescence is a process in which youth develop aspects of their personal and social identities by selecting and identifying with various role models. Given the historical, social, and economic limitations placed on Black manhood in America, the range of Black adult male role models available to adolescent boys may often be severely restricted. The developmental passage to adulthood becomes a confusing experience for many Black male youth because the evolution of gender appropriate roles and behaviors for Black men has often been stifled by historical and social powerlessness.

By the age of eighteen, the sum total of these impediments to psychosocial development in childhood and adolescence can often be seen in negative and self-destructive attitudes, behaviors, and values among young Black males. The impact of such factors has resulted in the direct negative consequences of educational underachievement, unemployment, delinquency, substance abuse, homicide, and incarceration in disproportionate numbers for Black male youth (Cordes, 1985; Gibbs, 1988).

Conclusion

While scores of Black male youth develop the survival strategies, coping mechanisms, and forms of resistance to successfully master the developmental tasks of childhood and adolescence, it must be understood that social and environmental forces have historically been stacked against the psychosocial development of Black males. For this reason, those committed to the empowerment of Black male youth must first understand the dimensions of Blacks' psychosocial development. It is important to appreciate that these dimensions are complex and challenging in a society that has historically placed the Black male at social and economic risk.

REFERENCES

Chestang, L. W. (1980). Character development in a hostile environment. In M. Bloom (Ed.), *Life span development* (pp. 40-50). New York: Macmillan Publishing Co.

Cordes, C. (1985, January). Black males face high odds in a hostile society. *APA Monitor*, pp. 9-11, 27.

Crawley, B., & Freeman, E. M. (1993). Themes in views of the life of older and younger African American males. *Journal of African American Male Studies, 1*, 15-29

Erikson, E. (1950). *Childhood and society.* New York: Norton.

Gibbs, J. T. (1988). Young Black males in America: Endangered, embittered, and embattled. In J.T. Gibbs (Ed.), *Young, Black and Male in America: An endangered species*, pp. 1-36. New York: Auburn House.

Goldberg, H. (1976). *The hazards of being male: Surviving the myth of masculine privilege.* New York: New American Library.

Grier, W. H., & Cobbs, P. M. (1968). *Black rage.* New York: Basic Books.

Havighurst, R. J. (1972). *Developmental tasks and education, (3rd ed.).* New York: McKay.

Hernton, C. (1965). *Sex and racism in America*. New York: Grove.

Hilliard, A. G. (1985). A framework for focused counseling on the African American man. *Journal of Non-White Concerns in Personnel and Guidance, 13,* 72-78.

Kohlberg, L. (1966). Moral education in the schools: A developmental view *School Review,* 74, 1-30.

Lee, C. C. (1990). Black male development: Counseling the "native son." In D. Moore & F. Leafgren (Eds.) *Problem solving strategies and interventions for men in conflict,* pp. 125-137. Alexandria, VA: AACD.

Madhubuti, H. (1990). *Black men: Obsolete, single, dangerous? Afrikan American families in transition: Essays in discovery, solution and hope.* Chicago: Third World Press.

Myers, H. F., & King, L. M. (1980). Youth of the Black underclass: Urban stress and mental health. *Fanon Center Journal, 1,* 1-27.

Piaget, J. (1970). *Science of education and the psychology of the child.* New York: Onion Press.

Pleck, J. H., & Sawyer, J. (Eds.). (1974). *Men and masculinity.* Englewood Cliffs, NJ: Prentice-Hall.

Staples, R. (1978). Masculinity and race: The dual dilemma of Black men. *Journal of Social Issues, 34,* 169-183.

Staples, R. (1983). *Black masculinity: The Black male's role in American society.* San Francisco: Black Scholar Press.

Staples, R. (1987). Black male genocide: A final solution to the race problem in America. *The Black Scholar, 18,* 2-11.

Taylor, R. L. (1977). Socialization to the Black male role. In D. Y. Wilkinson & R. L. Taylor (Eds.), *The black male in America: Perspectives on his status in contemporary society,* pp.1-6. Chicago: Nelson-Hall.

Thomas, A., & Sillen, S. (1972). *Racism & psychiatry.* Seacacus, NJ: The Citadel Press.

Washington, V., & Lee, C.C. (1982). Teaching and counseling Black males in grades K to 8. *Journal of the National Association of Black Social Workers, 13,* 25-29. Wilkinson, D. Y. & Taylor, R. L. (1977). *The Black male in America: Perspectives on his status in contemporary society.* Chicago: Nelson-Hall.

CHAPTER THREE

AFRICAN/AFRICAN-AMERICAN CULTURE: ITS ROLE IN THE DEVELOPMENT OF BLACK MALE YOUTH

Introduction

Anyone seeking to understand the development of Black male youth must consider the cultural dynamics that shape that development. Empowerment initiatives should be predicated on an understanding of Black culture and its crucial role in fostering development. Black educators and psychologists have concluded that there are aspects of the Black cultural experience in America that have evolved out of African tradition. These aspects have a significant relationship with mental health and psychosocial development (Cross, 1974; Harper, 1973; Nobles, 1972; Pasteur & Toldson, 1982; White & Parham, 1990). These conclusions have led to a framework for understanding Black behavior and personality.

An examination of core Black culture (i.e. the attitudes, behaviors, and values which have developed in relatively homogeneous Black communities where rudimentary Afrocentric ways of life have been preserved to a great extent), will reveal that Americans of African descent have developed a unique world-view. This view of the world reflects the historical experience of Black people in America and is based on African-oriented philosophical assumptions. This world-view encompasses a cultural tradition reflected in the concept of "Black Expressiveness" (Pasteur & Toldson,

1982). Black expressiveness can be found in the expressive behaviors and cultural life of people world-wide who trace their roots to Africa. For Black Americans, this concept can be considered the vestigial remains of an African personality distilled through the American experience.

Five important dimensions characterize Black expressiveness. Each of these contribute significantly to Black mental health and psychosocial development. These dimensions represent a healthy fusion of the cognitive, affective, and behavioral aspects of personality. First, Black expressiveness is characterized by a high degree of emotional energy exhibited in interpersonal interactions and behavior. Second, it is marked by a propensity among Black people to exhibit real, honest, and authentic behavior in all human relationships. Third, style and flair are hallmarks of this phenomenon. This is often seen in the creative manner Black people have found to put their personalities on display. Fourth, it is seen in the language and speech traditions of Black people, which are direct, creative, and communicate both information and significant affect. Finally, it is characterized by expressive movement. This is an ability to integrate thought, feeling, and movement into a whole and respond to the environment in a spontaneous fashion.

Collectively, these five dimensions represent the healthy manifestation of Black personality. Black expressiveness is a desirable psychosocial construct and the basis of positive attitudes, values, and behavior. However, when it has been considered in a traditional European/European-American psychoeducational context, it has often been viewed as deviant, deficient, or pathological.

Black Culture and Male Socialization

The cultural traditions inherent in Black expressiveness are the foundation of Black male socialization. From an early age, scores of Black male youth are socialized into these cultural traditions in the home and the Black community at large (Allen, 1981; Staples, 1982; Wilson, 1987). These socializing agents transmit the traditions that comprise the world-view of young Black males.

A synthesis of this cultural tradition is readily apparent in the personalities of Black males from an early age. It can be considered the basis of a distinctive Black male culture (Hale, 1982; Majors & Billson, 1992). Majors and Billson (1992), refer to these personality dynamics as *"cool pose"* and consider them to be the cornerstone of Black male identity. *"Cool Pose"* is a ritualized expression of masculinity involving behavior, speech, and posturing that communicates strength and control among Black males. Observing Black male youth, these dynamics become apparent in the following ways:

Social behavior. There is a dynamism associated with the social behavior of young Black males. Their peer group interactions, for example, are often characterized by high levels of energy. These interactions tend to be very physical and demonstrative. "Woofing" (engaging in aggressive verbal interchanges) or roughhousing with one another, young Black males use their bodies in expressive ways. One such example of this expressive body use is the cultivating of distinctive handshakes among young Black males.

In settings where limits are set on behavioral expressiveness, such as school, the cultural dynamism of Black males is often difficult to hold in check for extended periods of time. Young Black males need to physically respond to intellectual, affective, or behavioral stimuli.

Authenticity. There is a propensity among young Black males to exhibit real, honest, and authentic behavior in all interactions. This is seen as "being for real" or "telling it like it is." They tend not to stifle their true thoughts, feelings, or behaviors in most social situations. While such authenticity may not always be appreciated or understood by others, Black males tend to cut to the heart of a matter with their genuineness.

Language and Speech. The language and speech of young Black males is highly expressive and exhibits considerable creativity. Colorful slang expressions, *"woofing,"* playing the *"dozens,"* and the popular *"rap"* vernacular are innovative ways that have been developed to communicate both the trivial and the profound. Often these expressive linguistic traditions are used in order to diffuse tension between young males that could lead to physical aggression. For example, the often harsh verbal volleying that accompanies "woofing," can prevent two Black males from coming to physical blows.

Style. Young Black males find creative ways to put their personalities on display. One has only to examine the style and flair exhibited by Black males on the basketball court, the swagger associated with walking, hats worn at a jaunty angle, fancy sneakers, or flashy articles of clothing , to appreciate the expressiveness inherent in the style of young Black males. These artifacts are attempts to strike a "cool pose" and make a proud statement about oneself.

These personality dynamics are healthy manifestations of Black culture on the part of young Black males. As Majors and Billson (1992) suggest, these cultural manifestations serve as an important coping mechanism. Rather than confront the traditions of racism and oppression, which characterize the Black experience in America, with anger and frustration, Black males have released their tension by channeling energies into the development of expressive personality dynamics. Therefore, such dynamics have contributed significantly to Black male survival.

Black Male Culture and the School Setting

While many of the expressive dimensions discussed above may be characteristic of young Black females, as well as youth from other ethnic backgrounds, their manifestation among Black males has generally been the most misunderstood in the

American social arena. In schools, for example, it is not unusual for the dimensions of Black male culture to be seen as a major threat to the established social order. It has been alleged that educators have predetermined negative views concerning Black male culture and may expect to encounter difficulties in their interactions with Black male students because of them (Washington & Lee, 1982). These views, and the actions educators take related to them, are a major reason why scores of young Black males end up mislabeled or negatively tracked in the educational system. Engaging in normal, healthy Black male behavior in school, therefore, can often have negative consequences for male youth.

Educators and Black Culture: New Perspective on Male Empowerment

A new perspective on Black male empowerment is needed. Empowerment interventions for Black male youth must be implemented with the knowledge that Black culture fosters attitudes, behaviors, and values that are positive and promote the development of young males within it. Empowerment interventions, therefore, must be undertaken from a perspective that focuses on the development of male youth by promoting Black cultural expressiveness. Educators and others must be armed with a solid Black cultural knowledge base to address effectively the educational challenges facing young Black males.

REFERENCES

Allen, W. R. (1981). Moms, dads, and boys: Race and sex differences in the socialization of male children. In L. E. Gary (Ed.), *Black men.*, (pp. 99-114). Beverly Hills, CA: Sage Publications.

Cross, A. (1974). The Black experience: Its importance in the treatment of Black clients. *Child Welfare, 52*, 158-166.

Hale, J. E. (1982). *Black children: Their roots, culture, and learning styles.* Provo, Utah: Brigham Young University Press.

Harper, F. (1973). What counselors must know about the social sciences of Black Americans. *Journal of Negro Education, 42*, 109-116.

Majors, R. & Billson, J. M. (1992). *Cool pose: The dilemmas of Black manhood in America.* New York: Simon and Schuster.

Nobles, W. (1972). African philosophy: Foundations for a Black psychology. In R. L. Jones (Ed.), *Black psychology.* New York: Harper & Row.

Pasteur, A. B., & Toldson, I. L. (1982). *Roots of soul: The psychology of Black expressiveness.* Garden City: Anchor Press/Doubleday.

Staples, R. (1982). *Black masculinity.* San Francisco: Black Scholar Press.

Washington, V., & Lee, C. C. (1982). Teaching and counseling Black males in grades K to 8. *Journal of the National Association of Black Social Workers, 39*, 25-29.

White, J. L. & Parham, T. A. (1990). *The psychology of Blacks: An African-American perspective (2nd ed.).* Englewood Cliffs, NJ: Prentice Hall.

Wilson, A. N. (1978). *The developmental psychology of the Black child.* New York: Africana Research Publications.

CHAPTER FOUR

"THE YOUNG LIONS": AN EDUCATIONAL EMPOWERMENT PROGRAM FOR BLACK MALES IN GRADES 3-6

RONALD

Ronald is a nine year old Black male in the fourth grade at a public elementary school. He comes to school every day proudly wearing the latest fashions including a cap and expensive sneakers with the laces untied. Most days when he comes into the classroom, his female teacher confronts him about removing his cap and tying his shoelaces. Ronald usually storms over to the other side of the room, mumbles under his breath, and grudgingly removes his cap.

As the morning's instruction proceeds, Ronald occupies his time interacting with the other boys who sit around him. He enjoys talking with them, giving them "high fives," and generally joking and teasing with them. The teacher perceives Ronald to be inattentive and the instigator of most of this activity. She proceeds to reprimand him about his behavior.

When the teacher reprimands Ronald, he gets upset at her protestations, claiming that she is picking on him. She claims that he is not paying attention. However, when she presses him about the topic under class discussion, he is

able to respond correctly. In fact, Ronald claims that he has raised his hand several times that morning, but that the teacher ignores him.

The teacher notices again that Ronald's shoelaces are still untied. She sternly orders him to tie the laces. Ronald staunchly refuses, stating that this is the way they are supposed to be worn. She states that in her classroom, shoelaces will be tied. Again, she orders him to lace the shoes and moves toward Ronald, placing her hand on his shoulder and looking him squarely in the face.

At this point, Ronald jerks away from the teacher and shouts, "Don't be touchin' me Bitch!" He forcefully walks away from the teacher, picks up a book and flings it across the classroom. The teacher then orders Ronald to go to the principal's office.

The issues in Ronald's case are representative of those confronting many Black male youth in contemporary elementary schools. It must be understood that elementary education in this country is an enterprise greatly influenced by White, middle-class, female culture. The teaching-learning process at this educational level overwhelmingly represents aspects of this culture. The early years of school for young Black males, therefore, are often characterized by dissimilarity and imbalance. Confronted daily with attitudes, behaviors, and values of teachers, who in many instances are unaware of or insensitive to the personality and behavioral dynamics of Black male culture, bright and capable boys such as Ronald can become alienated from the educational process at an early age (Patton, 1981). A review of this case makes it is easy to speculate that after a number of punitive visits to the principal's office, precipitated by the clash of teacher-student cultural realties, Ronald will be negatively labeled and ultimately consigned to a failure track.

Those committed to Black male empowerment could work to prevent alienation on Ronald's part with programmed intervention at several levels. For example, Chapter 7 gives direction for consulting with teachers to increase their awareness, knowledge, and skills for successfully teaching Black males. This chapter, however, presents an intervention program for promoting educational empowerment among Black males at the elementary level, specifically grades 3 thorough 6. It is designed to be initiated at the third grade level because evidence suggests that educational and social problems for Black children begin to manifest themselves by this time (Morgan, 1980).

Background for the Program

Educators have long stressed the importance of Black consciousness or self-identity to the psychosocial development of Black children (Barnes, 1991; Clark & Clark, 1947; White & Johnson, 1980). Within this context, efforts have been undertaken, in both teaching and counseling, to develop a curriculum that promotes the self-concept of Black children by emphasizing African/African American culture and history (Hale, 1982; Lee, 1989; Lee & Lindsey, 1985).

Kunjufu (1986) conceptualizes a framework for developing a relevant empowerment initiative for young Black males that incorporates African/African- American culture. He advocates initiating intervention models which encompass the spirit and intent of traditional programs, such as the Boy Scouts and Big Brothers, for the protection and development of young Black males. The objectives of such models should include skill development, Black history, male socialization, recreation, and adult male role models. Kunjufu has identified the Swahili word *"Simba,"* which means *"Young Lion,"* as a generic name for such programs. This chapter describes a program developed, using Kunjufu's proposed framework, as an educational empowerment experience that can be included as part of an elementary school curriculum.

The Program

The program is called *"The Young Lions"* and is a multisession, psychoeducational empowerment experience for Black males in grades 3 through 6. It provides the opportunity for participants to spend quality educational time during the school day with Black men who serve as role models/mentors. The program stresses the development of the motivation and skills necessary for academic success, the development of positive and responsible social behavior, an understanding and appreciation of Black history and culture, and the modeling of positive Black male images.

While an experience such as this would be beneficial for most Black boys in grades 3 through 6, efforts should be made to insure that those who are experiencing significant academic and/or social frustration in the classroom, such as Ronald in the above case study, are given priority. A major goal of the program is to help boys labeled "at-risk" avoid those problems which often lead to their ultimate failure in school.

Prior to the start of such a program, parents and school officials should be made aware of the rationale for conducting an educational experience separated by ethnicity and gender in the school setting. An important argument for conducting such an experience is that it is not unusual for Black males to be set apart in the school setting, usually for special education classes or for disciplinary reasons. Often the number of Black male youth separated for such purposes is disproportionate to their numbers in the total school population. Therefore, separating Black males for an experience such as this, which is proactive and developmental, should be welcomed as a way to promote academic success and decrease disciplinary involvement.

If such a program is to be successful, competent Black men must be included as role models/mentors. This is important because of the paucity of Black male educators in elementary schools. These role models/mentors and their interactions with the boys, therefore, must be the cornerstone of the program. Chapter 6 provides guidelines for getting concerned Black men involved in such a program.

An important feature of the experience is the use of selected Black art forms. Specifically these include music, poetry, folklore, and culture-specific curriculum materials used as educational aids. It has been suggested that such curriculum materials and aesthetic dimensions be incorporated into psychoeducational interventions with Black students as a way to facilitate personal and social growth (Lee & Lindsey, 1985; Lee, 1989; Pasteur & Toldson, 1982).

The program is presented here as a year-long experience. It may however be shortened and intensified according to individual preferences and institutional considerations. The general framework of the program is to assign each boy a role model/mentor for approximately one hour twice a week. Depending upon the number of male volunteers, however, it may be necessary to have a role model/mentor work with more than one boy at a time. In such cases, attempts should be made to keep the student-role model/mentor ratio at 2 to 1. The one-hour sessions should be devoted to working on homework assignments, improving reading and mathematics skills, and discussing personal-social concerns.

The role model/mentors should be responsible for maintaining contact with classroom teachers to ensure a degree of congruity between program activities and classroom learning experiences. In addition, they should make periodic contact with parents regarding the boys' progress in the program.

Twice-a-month, all role models/mentors and their students should gather together in a one-hour session for academic and social-enrichment activities. These activities should focus on self-concept enhancement and the improvement of academic and social behavior. The facilitation of this large group experience should be shared by the role models/mentors. This chapter provides a description of the orientation session that launches the entire program, its general purpose, methods of facilitation, and intended educational experiences for these large group sessions.

"THE YOUNG LIONS":

AN EDUCATIONAL EMPOWERMENT PROGRAM FOR BLACK MALES IN GRADES 3-6.

GOAL OF THE PROGRAM

To help Black males in grades 3 through 6 develop motivation and skills for academic success, positive and responsible social behavior, and an understanding and appreciation of Black culture and history. This is accomplished by providing the opportunity for boys to spend quality educational time during the school day with an older Black male who serves as a role model/mentor. The role model/ mentor models positive Black male attitudes, behaviors, and values.

Program Orientation

Goal: This session will orient participants to the program, introduce the role models/mentors, and pair up men and boys.

Methods of Facilitation

　　1) Explain to boys the purpose and nature of the program: they will work with a role model/ mentor for one hour twice a week on homework assignments, reading and mathematics skills, and personal-social issues. Twice-a-month, they will gather in a large group session for social-enrichment activities. It is important to emphasize to the boys that to be chosen for participation in the program is an *honor.*

2) Introduce the role models/mentors and explain their role. Stress that these men bring much wisdom and knowledge and are to be considered as *"respected elders."* As such, they are to be treated with honor and respect.

3) Have each boy introduce himself to the group.

4) Discuss the importance of the name of the program: ***"The Young Lions."*** Explain the notion of the lion as "king of the animals" and its traditional importance to African people as a symbol of strength and courage. Introduce how this program will help these young males to develop the strength and courage of young lions through achieving school success. Tell them that when they gather together as a group they will be referred to as *"Pride,"* which is a company of lions. Their group meetings, therefore, will be referred to as *"a gathering of the pride."*

5) Make student-role model/mentor assignments. Allow time for participants and their role model/ mentor to get acquainted.

• After this session, participants begin twice-a-week one-on-one or small group educational enhancement sessions with role models/mentors. The following sections describe the bi-monthly communal gatherings of all participants and role models/mentors.

"A GATHERING OF THE PRIDE"

Session 1   *Pride*

Goal: To provide participants with an opportunity to enhance their self-esteem.

Methods of Facilitation

1) Find a picture of a pride of lions to put on the door of the meeting room with the message: "Do Not Disturb: Young Lions in Session." (Use this whenever the group meets).

2) Ask participants to share impressions of lions they have seen on television, in motion pictures, at the zoo, etc. Record impressions on chalkboard or newsprint.Reiterate to participants that a company of lions is called a *"pride."* Explain that the word *pride* also has another important meaning. Conduct the *"What Is Pride"* exercise from the book, *Pride: A Handbook of Activities to Motivate the Teaching of Elementary Black Studies* (Watson, 1971). Write the meaning of the word "pride" on the board or newsprint: e.g., "delight *or elation arising from some act, possession or relationship"* (Webster, 1990). Have participants read this meaning out loud. Translate the definition into terms that can be readily understood by the group.

Questions for Group Discussion:

a. How many of you have pride?

b. What do you have pride in?

c. What is "Black Pride?"

d. What kinds of things can you do in school to develop pride in yourself?

Intended Educational Experiences

1) To help participants begin increasing their self-esteem.

2) To continue developing a sense of brotherhood among men and boys.

> 3) To have participants begin to develop a sense of personal pride.

Session 2   *When I Grow Up*

Goal: To explore future goals and expectations and what it will take to realize them.

Methods of Facilitation

> 1) Introduce the concept of the *Twenty-First Century*. Explain to the group the significance of the start of a new century. Stress the fact that they will be young men in the twenty-first century.

Questions for Group Discussion:

> a. How old will you be in the year 2010, 2020, 2030, etc.?
> b. Where do you think you will be living in those years? Will you be married? Will you have children?
> c. What kind of job will you have?
> d. How can doing well in school now help you when you are grown up in the twenty-first century?
> e. What things that you are learning in school now will help you in the twenty-first century?

Intended Educational Experiences

> 1) To have participants begin focused thinking about their futures.
> 2) To impress upon group members the relationship between present academic achievement and future goals.

Sessions 3 - 5   *Bad Times*

Goals: 1) To have the boys critically examine the dynamics of the academic and social problems confronting them as students, and 2) to have them develop proactive strategies and techniques for confronting these challenges.

Methods of Facilitation

    1) Play the recording *"Bad Times"* by the vocal group Tavares. In conjunction with the lyrics of this song, develop a series of situations for participants to role play that involve problems they face in the school setting. For example, role plays involving confrontations with teachers. Using these role plays, help the boys develop strategies for dealing effectively with these problems.

Questions for Group Discussion:

    a. What are some problems that you have in school? Why do you think you have these problems?

    b. Do you feel that you are treated differently from the Black girls or the White children in school?

    c. Most of the time, when you get into trouble at school, is it your fault or do you think that the teachers are just picking on you?

    d. What can you learn from having bad times at school?

    e. What can you do to keep from having bad times at school?

    2) Have participants read aloud the poem *"Mother to Son"* by Langston Hughes. This poem is a mother's exhortation to her son not to give up because he experiences bad times and hardship in life. Explain the poem's message and discuss it with the participants.

Saving the Native Son:
Empowerment Strategies for Young Black Males

Intended Educational Experiences
1) To help boys develop awareness, knowledge, and skills in problem-identification and constructive problem-solving.
2) To help participants gain an appreciation of Black male struggle and persistence.

Session 6

** **Game Day** (** A session such as this could be repeated throughout the program.)

Goal: To increase the level of sportsmanship and constructive physical activity among participants.
Method of Facilitation
Engage in some form of physical activity. For example, organize a group basketball game: boys vs. men. Discuss with the group why it is important to have a strong body, as well as a strong mind.
Intended Educational Experiences
1) To have participants become aware of the importance of physical fitness and its relationship to success,
2) To enhance the sense of community among boys and men by having them interact outside of an educational context.

Sessions 7 - 9

Heroes, Part 1: "Great Kings of Africa"

Goal: To have participants gain a greater appreciation for and understanding of the accomplishments of their African forefathers.

Methods of Facilitation

1) Play the recording, *"Waaslu,"* by Olatunji (1970) or similar African music and ask boys about their impressions of Africa.

2) Explore with the group the following questions: *"How many of you have ever thought that your ancestors could have been kings? What is a king? What does a king do?"*

3) From encyclopedias and resources on Africa (e.g. *" Great Kings of Africa "* series from Anheuser-Busch, Inc.), prepare information on great African kings to share and discuss with participants, e.g. Mansa Musa-King of Mali, Osei Tutu-King of Asante, and Askia Muhammed Toure-King of Songhay.

Question for Group Discussion:

When these kings were boys your age, they were usually a prince. What kinds of things do you think a prince has to learn if he is to become a great king?

4. "KING FOR A DAY." In conjunction with this session, construct a king's crown. Explain to participants that a crown sets a king apart from the rest of the people and was the symbol of his power and authority. Boys should be accorded the honor of wearing the crown during succeeding sessions in recognition of outstanding school achievements.

Session 10   *Free to be Me*

Goal: To have participants personalize group activities experienced thus far, both as young Black males and as students.

Methods of Facilitation

1) Play the song *"Just Got to be Myself,"* by the Voices of East Harlem which deals with developing a sense of self-identity. Within the context of being young Black males explore the question, *"What does it mean to be yourself?"*

2) Ask boys, "How does it feel to be a young lion?" and "What have you learned from this group so far?" Record responses on chalkboard or newsprint. Discuss in greater depth any areas or concepts covered that remain unclear to group members.

3) To further the process of personalizing group experiences, consider again the word *"pride."* Ask, *"What does this word mean to you now?"* Ask again, *"What kinds of things can you do in school to develop pride in yourself?"*

Intended Educational Experiences

1) To have participants learn the importance of individuality.

2) To learn that success in school stems from a sense of pride in oneself.

Sessions 11 - 13

Heroes, Part 2: African American Men of Distinction

Goal: To have participants examine the boyhoods of famous Black American men in order to gain a greater appreciation for and understanding of the foundation for their accomplishments.

Methods of Facilitation

1) Have participants read aloud the poem *"I, Too, Sing America"* by Langston Hughes. This poem is a young Black boy's strong declaration that he will prevail against segregation and take his

rightful place in American society. Discuss the meaning of the poem for Black boys today.

2) Read, or have participants read, brief biographic information focusing on the boyhoods of famous Black Americans, such as Louis Armstrong, Arthur Ashe, Guy Bluford, Ralph Bunche, George Washington Carver, Frederick Douglass, W. E. B. DuBois, Alex Haley, Langston Hughes, Jesse Jackson, Martin Luther King, Jr., Jackie Robinson, Booker T. Washington, and Malcolm X.

Questions for Group Discussion:

a. What happened to these men when they were boys that helped to make them famous?

b. How were their boyhoods like yours?

c. How were their boyhoods different from yours?

d. What can you learn about "pride" from these boy hoods?

3) Show excerpts of the Gordon Parks film, *"The Learning Tree."* This is an autobiographical film directed by the famous Black photographer which traces a year in the life of a young boy. During this year, he learns about love, fear, racial injustice, and his own capacity for honor. Discuss with the participants the differences and similarities between their lives and the life of the young boy in the film.

Intended Learning Experiences

1. To have participants learn about the importance of Black males in American history and culture.

2. To have participants gain an appreciation for the universality of boyhood experiences.

3. To have participants gain a greater understanding of the dynamics of school success.

4. To have participants gain a greater understanding of the connection between early educational success and achievement in later life.

Sessions 14 & 15

Heroes, Part 3: African American Men of Distinction (Continued)

Goals: 1) to make participants aware of occupations of contemporary Black men, and 2) to impress upon them how education is important to obtaining a place in the world of work.

Methods of Facilitation

1. Do a variation of the *"On Being Black"* exercise from Watson (1971). Prepare a questionnaire about Black men in various occupational roles, e.g.:

Do you know a Black man who is an auto mechanic?	Y N
Do you know a Black man who is a dentist?	Y N
Do you know a Black man who is a plumber?	Y N
Do you know a Black man who is a teacher?	Y N
Do you know a Black man who is a pilot?	Y N
Do you know a Black man who is a custodian?	Y N
Do you know a Black man who is a basketball player?	Y N
Do you know a Black man who is a doctor?	Y N
Do you know a Black man who is a musician?	Y N

2. Have participants complete the questionnaire. When finished, total the number of people who know men in each category. Discuss the following questions, "When these men were your age, do you think they were good students in school?" "Why?"

3. List the following school subjects on the board or newsprint: Reading, Math, Language Arts, Spelling, Science, Art, Music, and Social Studies. Review each subject and have participants consider what subjects one would have to be good at to be a success in the listed occupations.

4. Play the "rap" recording *"Knowledge is King"* * by Kool Moe Dee. Discussed what is meant by the term *"knowledge is king."*

Intended Learning Experiences

1. To have participants learn about the importance of Black males in the contemporary American workforce.

2. To have participants gain a greater understanding of the dynamics of school success.

3. To have participants gain a greater understanding of early educational success to future occupational success.

    * *Cautionary note: While "rap," as an art form, has its roots in the oral tradition of African/African-American people, caution is suggested when using it in empowerment programs. The lyrics of many rap recordings contain language that may not be suitable for young children.*

Sessions 16 & 17   *Eyes on the Prize*

Goal: To have participants synthesize their learning and experiences from the program into personal action plans.

Methods of Facilitation

1) Play the "rap" recording *"Keep Your Eyes on the Prize,"* by Young MC. Discuss with the participants the meaning of "keeping your eyes on the prize." To focus on the notion of school success ask, *"What 'prize' should you have your eye on in school."*

2) Ask *"How are you going to win your prize?"* On the board, or on newsprint, place the following:

WINNING THE PRIZE

I am a young lion. I have pride in myself. I will keep my eyes on the prize and do well in school. I will be a success.
* When I am in school I will

_____.

* When I am at home I will

_____.

Have the participants fill in the blanks with the things they must do, both at home and in school, to succeed academically and socially.

3) Have each participant develop a personal action plan by filling out an individual sheet with his ideas for winning the prize. Have both the boy and his role model/mentor sign the sheet. Encourage them to put it up in a prominent place at home. Share a copy with participants' teachers and parents.

4) Ask each participant to share with the group why he feels that he will "win the prize" and be a success in school.

5) As a final activity, have the group attempt to compose their own "rap" about academic success.

Intended Educational Experience

To have participants learn that academic and social success requires personal commitment and action.

Session 18 *Young Lions: Black and Proud*

Goal: To terminate the group by reinforcing and personalizing activities and experiences.

Methods of Facilitation

1) Note that this will be the last gathering of the pride. Play the recording *"Say It Loud (I'm Black and I'm Proud)"* by James Brown. Consider again the word *"pride."* Ask, *"What does this word mean to you now?"* Ask again, *"What kinds of things can you do in school to develop pride in yourself?"*

2) Ask the boys, *"Now that we have come to the last session, how does it feel to be a young lion?"*, *"How are you like a lion?"*, and *"What have you learned from this group?"* Record responses on chalkboard or newsprint.

3) Place the term "Pride of Lions" with the suggested accompanying words on the board or newsprint in the following manner:

P roud		**L** eaders
R espectful		**I** ndustrious
I nitiative	OF	**O** bedient
D iligent		**N** ever Give Up
E xcellence		**S** uccessful

Explain the meaning of each word and its importance to a young lion. Duplicate this and give one to each participant. Encourage them to place it next to their action plan in a prominent place at home.

4) To reinforce the transfer of group experiences to school success, play the recording *"Ain't No Stopping Us Now,"* by McFadden and Whitehead. Discuss the inspirational meaning it brings to the lives of young Black males.

5) Conclude with a small celebration with food and music.

Saving the Native Son:
Empowerment Strategies for Young Black Males

Intended Educational Experiences
1. To help participants culminate the process of increasing their self-esteem.
2. To reinforce the notion of commitment to school success
3. To enhance the sense of brotherhood between boys and role models/mentors.

CONCLUDING PROGRAM

Goal: To honor participants for completing the program.

Method of Facilitation

Conduct some type of concluding program to celebrate successful completion of the program and to reinforce group experiences. Encourage parents, teachers, and administrators to participate in the group participants' celebration.

Sample Program

WELCOME & AFRICAN GREETING
......................A ROLE MODEL/MENTOR & BOY
SONG...BLACK NATIONAL ANTHEM
REMARKS ABOUT THE GROUP EXPERIENCE
......................A ROLE MODEL/MENTOR
INTRODUCTION OF ROLE MODELS/MENTORS ....BOYS
INTRODUCTION OF BOYS...........................ROLE MODELS/MENTORS
"REFLECTIONS ON BEING YOUNG LIONS"...............................BOYS

P roud	**L** eaders
R espectful	**I** ndustrious
I nitiative of	**O** bedient
D iligent	**N** ever give up
E xcellence	**S** uccessful

(Group members stand up and explain to the audience the importance of these words to young lions)

GROUP MEMBERS THEN RECEIVE CERTIFICATES AND A
TOKEN SYMBOLIZING THE COMPLETION OF THE PROGRAM
FROM ROLE MODELS/MENTORS. (*Certificates might have a picture
of a lion attached to it. An excellent token is a candle, symbolizing the
light of knowledge. Boys should be told to keep the candle in a safe
place and burn it on the day they graduate from high school in recognition
of their educational success.*)
POETRY READING: "To a Negro Boy Graduating" by Eugene T.
Maleska...ROLE MODEL/MENTOR

CLOSING REMARKS

After the program ends, the participants would benefit from
follow-up activities that would serve to reinforce the experience.
For example, there should be periodic follow-up sessions with
the role models/mentors. In conjunction with this, the role
models/mentors should continue consulting with teachers,
administrators, and parents to monitor participants' academic
and social progress. Additionally, participants should be
encouraged to become involved in leadership activities or be
given important responsibilities within the school (e.g. serving
on the student council, safety patrol, etc.).

Conclusion

Increasingly, words like *achievement* and *motivation* are not
associated with the "Ronalds" in America's elementary schools.
Instead, the contemporary elementary school experience sets
the tone for a lifetime of failure and frustration for scores of
Black males. If they are to have a chance at academic and
career success, Black male youth must have the opportunity to
master the basic skills and develop the motivation associated
with an elementary school education. The "Young Lions"
provides such an opportunity. It offers boys, such as Ronald,
who are at-risk for educational alienation, the chance to spend
quality educational time with adult Black male role models.

These role models are men who fully understand and appreciate the dynamics of Black male behavior and personality. The combination of individual tutoring and culturally relevant group guidance, which form the structure of the program, is designed to empower Black male youth for maximum academic and social success in the all-important elementary school years. Educators and others are urged to consider implementing such a program as an integral part of a comprehensive strategy for Black male empowerment.

Suggested Group Resources

Session 1

Watson, D. D. (1971). *Pride: A handbook of activities to motivate the teaching of elementary Black studies.* Stevensville, MI: Educational Service.

Webster's ninth new collegiate dictionary. (1989). Springfield, MA: Merriam-Webster.

Sessions 3-5

"Bad Times," by Tavares from the album *"Supercharged"* - Capitol Records, ST12026.

Hughes, L. (1970). Mother to son. In L. Hughes and A. Bontemps (Eds.), *The poetry of the Negro, 1746 to 1970* (p. 186). Garden City, NY: Doubleday.

Sessions 7-9

"Waaslu" by B. Olatunji, from the album *"More drums of passion"* - Columbia Records, C29307.

Anheuser-Busch, Inc. (1985). *"Great Kings of Africa."* St. Louis, MO.

Session 10

"Just Got to be Myself" by The Voices of East Harlem, from the album *"Can You Feel It"* - Just Sunshine Records, JSS-3504.

Sessions 11-13

Hughes, L. (1970). I, Too, Sing America. In L. Hughes and A. Bontemps (Eds.), *The poetry of the Negro, 1746 to 1970* (p. 182). Garden City, NY: Doubleday.

Parks, G. (1969). *The learning tree* [Film]. Hollywood, CA: Warner Brothers - Seven Arts, Inc.

Sessions 14 & 15

Watson, D. D. (1971). *Pride: A handbook of activities to motivate the teaching of elementary Black studies.* MI: Educational Service.

"Knowledge is King" by Kool Moe Dee from the album *"Knowledge is King"* - Zomba Recording Corp., 1182-4-J

Sessions 16 & 17

"Keep Your Eye on the Prize" by Young MC, from the album, *"Brainstorm"* - Capitol Records, C4-96337

Session 18

"Say It Loud (I'm Black and I'm Proud)" by James Brown, from the album, *"James Brown, 20 All Time Greatest Hits."* - Polydor Records, 314 511 326-4.

"Ain't No Stopping Us Now" by G. McFadden and J. Whitehead, from the album *"McFadden & Whitehead."* - Philadelphia International Records, J235800.

Concluding Program

Maleska, E.T. (1970). To a Negro Boy Graduating. In L. Hughes and A. Bontemps (Eds.), *The poetry of the Negro, 1746 to 1970* (p. 569). Garden City, NY: Doubleday.

REFERENCES

Barnes, E. J. (1991). The Black community as the source of positive self-concept for Black children: A theoretical perspective. In R. L. Jones (Ed.), *Black psychology* (3rd ed., pp. 667-692). Berkeley, CA: Cobb & Henry.

Clark, K. B., & Clark, M. P. (1947). Racial identification and preference in Negro children. In T.M. Newcomb & E.L. Hartley (Eds.), *Readings in socio-psychology* (pp. 169-178). New York: Holt, Rinehart and Winston.

Hale, J. E. (1982). *Black children: Their roots, culture, and learning styles.* Provo, Utah: Brigham Young University Press.

Kunjufu, J. (1986*). Countering the conspiracy to destroy Black boys (Vol. 2*) Chicago, IL: African American Images.

Lee, C. C. (1989). Counseling Black adolescents: Critical roles and functions for counseling professionals. In R. L. Jones (Ed.), *Black adolescents* (pp.298-308). Berkeley, CA: Cobb & Henry.

Lee, C. C. & Lindsey, C. R. (1985). Black consciousness development: A group counseling model for Black elementary school students. *Elementary School Guidance and Counseling, 19,* 228-236.

Morgan, H. (1980). How schools fail Black children. *Social Policy, 10,* 49-54.

Pasteur, A. B., & Toldson, I. L. (1982). *Roots of soul: The psychology of Black expressiveness.* Garden City, NY: Anchor Press/Doubleday.

Patton, J. M. (1981). The Black male's struggle for an education. In L. E. Gary (Ed.), *Black men.* Beverly Hills, CA: Sage Publications.

White, J. L., & Johnson, J. A. (1980). Awareness, pride, and identity: A positive educational strategy for Black youth. In R. L. Jones (Ed.), *Black psychology* (2nd ed., pp. 273-280). New York: Harper & Row.

CHAPTER FIVE

"BLACK MANHOOD TRAINING": AN EMPOWERMENT PROGRAM FOR ADOLESCENT BLACK MALES

MALIK

Malik is a thirteen-year-old Black male who is in the seventh grade at an urban junior high school. He lives in an apartment complex in a lower middle (working) class neighborhood with his mother and seven-year-old sister. Malik's parents have been divorced since he was six years old and he rarely sees his father.

Throughout his elementary school years, Malik was an honor-roll student. However, since starting junior-high school, his grades have dropped dramatically and he expresses no interest in doing well academically. He spends his days at school in the company of a group of seventh- and eighth- grade boys who are frequently in trouble with school officials.

Malik's mother must constantly take time off from her day job to come to school to meet with officials about Malik's poor academic performance and his problematic behavior. On one occasion, when she meets with Malik's counselor, she expresses her frustrations about her son.

She explains that she must work two jobs in order to support her children. Since she is often not home when the children get out of school and on the weekends, she depends on Malik to look after himself and his younger sister. She regrets not having the time to spend with Malik and confesses that she does not understand him anymore. She states that he does not talk to her and defies her. She says, "Something has gotten into him. He acts like he's grown."

Malik's mother goes on to say that recently he has been staying out late with his group of friends at the corner basketball court. She is upset because many of the boys and men who loiter around the basketball court have had run-ins with the police for petty thefts and drug dealing.

This case study represents the contemporary reality of many adolescent Black males. There are several important issues, which when considered collectively, suggest some major challenges to Malik's development. First, although his mother attempts to provide important developmental support for Malik, her efforts are limited due to the economic realities which compel her to spend a significant amount of time away from home. Related to this is the fact that in her absence, she has been forced to entrust household and child care responsibilities to Malik. In many respects Malik has been asked to shoulder a man's responsibilities.

Second, while Malik has distinguished himself as a student in the past, peer-group pressure has had a negative influence on his current academic performance. It is apparent that within his peer group, academic achievement is not valued, as is often the case in adolescence. Instead, the behavioral norm among Malik's friends appears to be attempting to push the limits of school authority. This type of behavior can have only negative consequences for Malik.

Third, and perhaps most significant, like many adolescent Black boys living in a female-headed, single-parent household,

Malik appears to be making the crucial and often difficult boyhood to manhood transition without the benefit of positive adult-male role modeling. While the men at the corner basketball court may provide Malik with role models, the nature of their influence on his development is highly questionable. At a time when he is asking the initial questions of manhood and seeking the right direction, there is no responsible male present to provide Malik with direction.

These issues suggest that Malik, like many of his contemporary adolescent Black male peers, may very well be on a fast track to educational and social failure. Without positive intervention, Malik could end up another negative Black male statistic, lost to the streets.

Given the dynamics of development suggested in Malik's case, school counseling professionals should seek to promote the attitudes and behaviors among adolescent Black males that will empower them to function at optimal psychosocial levels. In order to accomplish this, specific guidance is necessary to foster the awareness, knowledge, and skills of adolescent Black males.

This chapter examines a counseling program designed to promote the transition from boyhood to manhood for adolescent Black males. The original conception of the program was introduced by Lee (1987) as a group counseling experience for Black males in grades seven through twelve. Since its introduction, it has been adopted by middle-and secondary-school counselors around the country. While the program was originally conceived to be used in schools, it has been modified for implementation in a variety of settings, including fraternal organizations and community agencies. It has also been effectively implemented as a church-based experience (Lee & Woods, 1989).

The program is a developmental *"rites-of-passage"* experience that was developed within the context and spirit of a traditional African ritual known as *manhood training,* popularized by Alex Haley in his classic saga *Roots* (1976). Haley describes how during this training, adolescent boys in traditional African societies were isolated from their families for an extended period of time and given rigorous physical and mental training considered important in the development of men. This training was conducted by men from the community and had as its purpose the development of the attitudes and skills necessary to assume the responsibilities associated with the masculine role. If a boy successfully completed this training, he was formally acknowledged as a man among his people and accorded the rights and responsibilities of a man.

The program described in this chapter, developed within the context and spirit of this traditional African custom, demonstrates a way to help adolescent Black males assume positive masculine roles. The program is a multi-session, developmental, group guidance experience. Importantly, it redirects the focus of counseling strategies for adolescent Black males from a negative (reactive) stance to a positive (proactive) one. The program provides the opportunity for counselors to help adolescent Black males develop the attitudes and skills to effectively meet environmental challenges that often lead to problems in the school setting and beyond.

Like the elementary-school counseling experience presented in the previous chapter, this program makes use of selected Black art forms and culture-specific curriculum materials as educational aids in the guidance process. With this approach, the program stresses the development of strong Black men through a strengthening of body, mind, and soul. This is accomplished by promoting an understanding and appreciation of the Black man in African and African-American history and culture, by developing achievement motivation, by fostering positive and responsible behavior, and by modeling positive Black male images.

As with the elementary-school program, prior to selecting

group participants, counselors should consult with parents and school officials about the nature and purpose of the group. Attempts should be made to insure that group composition is heterogeneous with respect to socioeconomic status, academic-skill level, and extent of disciplinary involvement. Given the importance of modeling, an adult Black male facilitator is crucial for this experience. When necessary, concerted efforts should be made to include competent Black men from the school or community as group leaders.

The program is described here with major additions and modifications that have been made in its structure as a result of widespread use in schools and related settings. Readers are urged to consider the realities of their own institutional setting in establishing the number of sessions or the duration of the group experience. The program is presented as a guideline and, as such, it is open to additional modification. Its use is limited only by the bounds of individual creativity and imagination.

BLACK MANHOOD TRAINING: "BODY, MIND, AND SOUL"

GOAL OF THE PROGRAM

To help adolescent Black males develop positive masculine identities through a strengthening of body, mind, and soul. This strengthening is accomplished by promoting an understanding and appreciation of the Black man in history and culture, by developing achievement motivation, by fostering positive and responsible behavior, and by modeling positive Black-male images.

Introductory Sessions

Goal: To have group members become aware of the challenges associated with being Black *and* male and begin to reflect on the notion of masculinity from a Black perspective.

Saving the Native Son:
Empowerment Strategies for Young Black Males

Methods of Facilitation
1) Play the song *"What's Happening Brother?"* by Marvin Gaye. Lead a discussion of what is happening to *"brothers"* internationally, nationally, and locally— identify the global and specific challenges confronting Black males.
2) Lead a general discussion of the focal question of the program: *"What is a Strong Black Man?"* (i.e., A *"Brother?"*)
3. Explore with the group the images of Black men portrayed in the media (i.e. motion pictures and television)
   Have members identify these images as positive or negative. Using a chalkboard or newsprint, place the names of Black men considered by group members to represent positive images in one column and those considered to represent negative images in another. Have the group members explain their choices and ask them to defend their positive or negative selections.

Questions for Group Discussion:
a. What makes a man strong?
b. Who are some strong Black men that you know personally? What makes these men strong?
c. Do you think that you are strong? Why?

Intended Educational Experiences
1. To have group members become more aware of the challenges facing Black males internationally, nationally, and locally.
2. To have group members begin to analyze critically the image of Black men.
3. To have group members begin to examine the notion of masculinity and strength within a Black perspective. Play the song *"My Name is Man"* from the musical *"Don't Bother Me, I Can't Cope"* and

introduce the notion that masculinity comes from the strength of *Body, Mind, and Soul.* Begin to explore with the group members the notion of becoming a man by strengthening one's body, mind, and soul.

Sessions Related to the BODY

Goal: The goal of these sessions is to promote the concept that a strong Black man develops, protects, and cares for his body, i.e., *is physically healthy.*

Methods of Facilitation

1) Consult with physical-education teachers, coaches, and community recreation leaders to ensure that group members are involved in rigorous exercise or athletic programs. Explorewith group members why it is important for strong Black men to be physically fit.

2) Play recordings such as, *"The Bottle"* and *"Angel Dust"* by Gil Scott-Heron and explore with group participants Black male health hazards. Use recent data from sources such as the National Urban League, National Center for Health Statistics, and the U.S. Department of Health and Human Services to review the health status of Black men in contemporary America. Focus on issues such as Black-on-Black crime and the spread of AIDS among African American males.

Discussion Questions:

Is abuse of your body a sign of strength?

Does killing another "brother"prove that you are strong?

Is putting yourself in physical danger a sign of strength?

3. Play the recording, *"The Dude"* by Quincy Jones and discuss grooming and dress habits. Show the group participants pictures of well-

groomed, Black men taken from popular magazines and ask:

"What makes a real "Dude?"

"In terms of dress habits and grooming, how can you tell when a brother 'has his stuff together?'"

4. Discuss the importance of good nutrition and proper eating habits to a physically healthy Black man.

Intended Educational Experiences

1. To have group members become aware of the importance of developing and maintaining a strong body through physical exercise.

2. To have group members develop a *wellness mentality* which discourages activities that threaten physical health and well-being.

3. To have group members develop good grooming habits.

Sessions Related to the MIND

Goal: To promote the concept that a strong Black man develops and uses his *mind* to its fullest capacity by fostering the development of the attitude and skills necessary for optimal academic achievement.

Methods of Facilitation

1) To stress the historical importance of academic achievement to Black men, show excerpts from the Public Broadcasting System television series *"Eyes on the Prize,"* which chronicles the American Civil Rights Movement. Two excerpts of note are James Merideth's attempt to integrate the University of Mississippi in the 1960s and the efforts of Black students to enter Central High School in Little Rock, Arkansas in the 1950s. In addition, through biographic materials, examine the struggles of historical Black male figures, such as Frederick Douglass, to get an education.

After viewing the excerpts and reading biographic information, discuss with group members the idea that *strong Black men place a high value on education.*

Discussion Questions:

    a) What did you learn from "Eyes on the Prize" about strong Black men and education?

    b) What lessons can you learn from the life and struggles of men such as Frederick Douglass about strength, Black men, and education?

2) Conduct motivation sessions to facilitate the development of positive attitudes toward academic achievement. Develop group guidance activities focusing on inherent Black male potential that incorporate *historical* and *contemporary* references to the educational experiences of Black males. Expose the group members to both historical and contemporary *"respected elders,"* who can speak to them about the importance of education to Black-male survival.

    a) Respected Historical Elders: Have group members explore the *educational contributions* of Black men such as:

- George Washington Carver
- W.E.B. DuBois
- Booker T. Washington
- Paul Robeson
- Benjamin Mays
- Martin Luther King, Jr.

    b) Respected Contemporary Elders: Invite Black men from various sectors of the community to come to group sessions and share their *educational histories* with the participants. These might include the following:

- Student-athletes from local colleges

- Professional athletes who have succeeded athletically and academically
- Undergraduate and graduate students from local colleges
- Men from various sectors of the community who have successfully "made it"

3) Promote *"Scholastic Male-bonding"* among group members. Develop an *academic support network* within the group, the purpose of which is to have group members draw on each other's scholastic strengths in a collective effort to develop academic skills and competencies. Have members establish *group academic goals* and develop strategies for meeting them.

4) Coordinate tutorial help for group members, as needed.

5) Coordinate the development of skills in the following areas: Academic planning, study skills, time management, taking tests.

Questions for Group Discussion

a. Is education strength?

b. Why is it important for a strong Black man to be an educated man?

Intended Educational Experiences

1. To have group members become aware of the importance of developing and maintaining a strong mind.

2. To have group members learn from *"respected elders"* (both historical and contemporary) about the wisdom of academic achievement and its importance to Black male survival and success.

3. To have group members develop the attitudes and skills necessary for optimal academic achievement.

Sessions Related to the SOUL

Goal: To promote the concept that a strong Black man has an indomitable *spirit*. This is accomplished by fostering an understanding and appreciation of the

major life roles and responsibilities of the Black man.
Methods of Facilitation
1) Introduce the Black man's historical struggle to
survive and prevail by playing the recording, *"I Gotta
Keep Moving"* from the musical "Don't *Bother Me,
I Can't Cope"* and having the group read the poem,
"The Negro Speaks of Rivers," by Langston Hughes.
Discussion Question:
Given the challenges Black men have always had
to face, why have they survived?
2) Explore the various life roles that men can assume.
Have members choose the names of Black men who
fought for Black pride and glory from various
life roles. Each group member is to write a research
paper on the person(s) whose name he draws. After
researching, members present to the group
information about this person(s) that they feel
represents something about the *soul/spirit* of
the person(s) as a Black man. Black art forms
may be used in the presentation. Life roles and names
might include:
- Warriors: Great Kings of Africa, Hannibal,
Crispus Attucks, Nat Turner, Buffalo Soldiers,
Hell Fighters, Tuskegee Airmen, Benjamin O.
Davis, Colin Powell, Ezell Blair, Joseph
McNeil, David Richmond, Franklin McCain,
Colin Powell
- Athletes: Joe Louis, Jackie Robinson, Jesse Owens,
Muhammad Ali, Wendell Scott, Eddie Robinson,
Arthur Ashe, Doug Williams
- Artists: Henry O. Tanner, Richard Wright,
Ralph Ellison, Langston Hughes, James
Baldwin, James Van Der Zee, Ernie Barnes, Paul
Robeson, Sidney Poitier, Arthur Mitchell,
Alvin Ailey, Ray Charles, Wynton Marsalis,
Duke Ellington, Stevie Wonder, Denzel

Washington, Spike Lee
- Ministers: Adam Clayton Powell, Malcolm X, Martin Luther King, Jr.., Howard Thurman, Jesse Jackson, Desmond Tutu
- Entrepreneurs: Henry Parks, John Johnson, Edward Gardner, Earl Graves, Asa Spaulding, Berry Gordy
- Scientists: Lewis Lattimer, Charles Drew, Daniel Hale Williams, George Washington Carver, Guy Bluford, Ronald McNair, Fred Gregory
- Educators: Benjamin Mays, W.E.B. DuBois, Booker T. Washington, Kenneth Clark
- Politicians/Statesmen: Great Kings of Africa, Ralph Bunche, Tom Bradley, Andy Young, Wilson Goode, Harold Washington, William Gray, Coleman Young, Richard Hatcher, L. Douglas Wilder, David Dinkins, Jesse Jackson, Nelson Mandela
- Journalists: Frederick Douglass, Carl Rowan, Bryant Gumbel, John Johnson, Earl Graves, William Raspberry, Juan William, Ed Bradley, Chuck Stone, Alex Haley

3) Explore in depth the role of the Black man as father by examining the word *RESPONSIBILITY.* This stresses the notion that strong Black men take responsibility for their children. Play the recording *"Pappa Was a Rolling Stone,"* by the Temptations and discuss the negative father images in the song.

Questions for Group Discussion:
a. Does making babies make you a man?
b. Does fatherhood bring with it responsibilities? If so, what are some of these responsibilities?

c. Physically, you can now make babies, but are you
ready to be fathers?

4) Conduct a discussion of other key words related to
the soul/spirit of strong Black men:
MASCULINITY, STRENGTH, CHARACTER,
GIVING, CARING, SHARING, RESPECT, etc.

Questions for Group Discussion:

a. What do these words mean to you as young
Black men?

b. What do these words mean for your
relationships with other people as young Black
men (particularly Black women)?

Have the group read excerpts from the play
*"For Colored Girls Who Have Considered Suicide
When the Rainbow is Enuf,"* that focus on male-female
relationships and have the members examine these key words.

5) Paste pictures from magazines (e.g. *Ebony, Essence,
Jet*) that present varied images of Black men in many
life roles on newsprint. Present these pictures to the
group and examine how the soul/*spirit* of the Black
man is portrayed in each image.

6) Show the video presentation, *"Black, Male, and
Successful in America,"* which was produced by the
Alexandria, Virginia City Public Schools. This video
highlights the development of positive images and
life styles for Black males. Initiate a discussion of
the following questions related to the video:

a. What message about the soul or spirit of the
Black man do you get from this video?

b. As a result of watching this video, what kind
of things do you need to do to become a
successful Black man?

7) Facilitate personal explorations of various life roles
among group members by having them discuss
answers to the following questions: "How do you

see yourself as a _____?" (*son, boyfriend, brother, husband, father, uncle, etc.*)

Intended Counseling Experiences

1. To have group members gain an appreciation of the indomitable spirit of struggle and survival inherent in the soul of the strong Black man.
2. To have group members gain a sense of responsibility to self and others.
3. To have group members appreciate how *"soul power"* permeates the life roles of strong and successful Black men.
4. To have each group member gain a new perspective on his own soul as a young Black man.

Developing a Plan for Personal Action

Goal: To have participants synthesize important aspects of the group experience and set personal action goals derived from insights gained from the group.

Method of Facilitation

1. Play again the recording, *"My Name is Man"* from the musical *"Don't Bother Me, I Can't Cope"* and initiate a discussion of what the group experience has meant to each participant in terms of new insights into his body, mind, and soul as a young Black man.

Discussion Questions:

a. After all that you have experienced, What is a strong Black man? *(a "brother?")*
b. After being in this group, what kind of educational plans do you have?
c. After being in this group, what kind of career plans do you have?

Concluding Activities

THE "TEST OF WORTHINESS"

Goal: To "test" the body, mind, and soul of group participants to see if they possess the strength to be proclaimed as men.

Method of Facilitation

   1) Group members are given tests of body, mind, and soul, each of which they must "pass." *Note: The tests and the criteria for passing should be demanding, but flexible enough to insure that the majority of the participants will succeed.

   a. Test of the Body: e.g. Members must run a quarter of a mile on a track in a specified amount of time to prove that their bodies are strong.

   b. Test of the Mind: e.g. Members must complete a 100 problem math test and get a certain percentage correct to prove that their minds are strong.

   c. Test of the Soul: e.g. Members must participate in some responsible activity at school, at home, at church, or in the community to prove that their souls are strong.

Intended Educational Experience

To have group members culminate the process of developing their awareness, knowledge, and skills as young Black men.

INITIATION CEREMONY

Goal: To proclaim the manhood of group participants.

Method of Facilitation

   Conduct some type of manhood initiation or "rites-of-passage" ceremony to celebrate the manhood of the group members and to reinforce group experiences. Encourage parents and key men from the community to participate in the group participants' celebration.

Sample Initiation Ceremony

PROCESSIONAL...MEN & BOYS

WELCOME & AFRICAN MEDITATION...............GROUP LEADER
SONG..BLACK NATIONAL ANTHEM
REMARKS ABOUT THE GROUP EXPERIENCE
...................GROUP LEADER
INTRODUCTION OF RESPECTED ELDERS.
.................A GROUP MEMBER
"REFLECTIONS ON STRONG BLACK MANHOOD"
.................RESPECTED ELDERS

SPEAKER ON THE BODY.........e.g. A PHYSICIAN
SPEAKER ON THE MIND.........e.g. A TEACHER
SPEAKER ON THE SOUL.........e.g. A MINISTER

INTRODUCTION OF GROUP MEMBERS TO AUDIENCE
.................GROUP LEADER

"RITES OF PASSAGE"
(Each group member must stand up in front of the audience and state
what it means to him to be a strong Black man)

GROUP MEMBERS THEN RECEIVE CERTIFICATES OR SOME
TOKEN SYMBOLIZING THE COMPLETION OF MANHOOD
TRAINING FROM RESPECTED ELDERS

CLOSING REMARKS AND AFRICAN MEDITATION.
.................GROUP LEADER
RECESSIONAL...***MEN!***

Follow-Up Experiences

After the group experience and the initiation into manhood,
the participants would benefit from follow-up activities. These
would serve to reinforce the experience. Such activities might
include:

1) Periodic follow-up sessions with the leader.
2) Field trips to African/African-American cultural
institutions.

3) Spending time at work with responsible older Black men.
4) Participation in community service projects.
5) Participation in organized group interaction with their Black female counterparts and their male peers from other ethnic groups, as appropriate.
6) Serving as co-leaders for future manhood training groups.

Conclusion

The boyhood-to-manhood transition is a challenging developmental phenomenon. For adolescent Black males, such as Malik, the challenges associated with this phenomenon are often compounded by the absence of positive role models to point the way to manhood. With no one to model the attitudes, behaviors, and values of successful Black manhood, many adolescent males wander into self-defeating and self-destructive lifestyles.

The spirit and intent of *"Black Manhood Training"* is to point Black male youth in the direction of successful manhood. The program makes a concerted effort to involve successful Black men in the academic, career, and personal-social empowerment of adolescent males. Counselors attempting to incorporate such a program as part of a school counseling curriculum must keep in mind that while almost anyone can successfully raise a Black boy to adulthood, only a Black man can teach him how to be a man.

SUGGESTED RESOURCES

Introductory Sessions

"What's Happening Brother?" by Marvin Gaye, from the album *"What's Going On?"* - Motown Record Corp., HS1876.

"My Name is Man" by A. Wilkerson, from the Broadway cast album *"Don't Bother Me I Can't Cope."* - Polydor Records, PD-6013.

Body

"The Bottle" by Gil Scott-Heron, from the album, *"It's Your World."* - Arista Records, HS-226.

"Angel Dust" by Gil Scott-Heron, from the album, *"Secrets."* - Arista Records, HS-122.

"The Dude" by Quincy Jones, from the album, *"The Dude."* - A&M Records, SP-3721.

Mind

"Eyes on the Prize " [video recording]: America's civil rights years. Alexandria, VA: Corporation for Public Broadcasting.

Soul

"I Gotta Keep Moving" by Alex Bradford, from the Broadway cast album, *"Don't Bother Me I Can't Cope."* - Polydor Records, PD-6013.

Hughes, L. (1970). The Negro Speaks of Rivers. In L. Hughes and A. Bontemps (Eds.), *The poetry of the Negro, 1746 to 1970* (p. 187). Garden City, NY: Doubleday.

"Pappa Was a Rolling Stone" by The Temptations, from the album, *"The Motown Story."* - Motown Record Corporation, 6048ML5

Shange, N. (1975). *For colored girls who have considered suicide when the rainbow is enuf.* New York: Macmillan.

"Black, Male and Successful in America." Alexandria, Virginia Public Schools.

"My Name is Man" by A. Wilkerson, from the Broadway cast album, *"Don't Bother Me I Can't Cope."* - Polydor Records, PD-6013.

REFERENCES

Haley, A. (1976). *Roots.* Garden City: Doubleday.

Lee, C. C. (1987). Black manhood training: Group counseling for male Blacks in grades 7-12. *Journal for Specialists in Group Work, 12,* 18-25.

Lee, C. C., & Woods, C. W. (1989). *Black manhood training: Body, mind, and soul.* A church-based group counseling experience for adolescent Black males. Unpublished manuscript.

CHAPTER 6

TAPPING THE POWER OF RESPECTED ELDERS: ENSURING MALE ROLE MODELING FOR BLACK MALE YOUTH

School counseling professionals who want to help empower young Black males using models such as those described in chapters 4 and 5, must insure that competent Black men play a major role in the process. This is important for two reasons. First, only a Black man can teach a Black boy how to be a man. By virtue of attaining adult status as Black and male, he alone has the gender and cultural perspective to accurately address the boyhood-to-manhood transition issues of Black boys. While Black women and individuals of both sexes from other ethnic backgrounds can play a significant role in helping to empower young Black males, it is only a Black man who can model the attitudes and behaviors of successful Black manhood.

Second, there is a paucity of Black male educators in American schools. In reviewing ethnic/gender data for school personnel, Patton (1981) concluded that a majority of Black male students can spend an entire career in school and have very little interaction with a Black male teacher, counselor, or administrator until high school. Even then, as a result of the limited number of Black males at the secondary level, that interaction can be limited.

For these reasons, the challenge for many school counselors is to find ways to include Black men in empowerment interventions for Black male youth. Because the presence of

Black males as professionals in the school setting may be limited, counselors must be prepared to look beyond the school for nontraditional male educational resources. While the landscape in many Black communities may be dotted with men who are less than desirable role models, there are countless others whose achievements and experiences make them potential respected elders. These men can significantly influence the cognitive and affective development of young Black males (Washington & Lee, 1982). A concerted effort must be made to find them.

This chapter provides guidelines for getting concerned Black men involved in school-based interventions for the empowerment of young Black males. The focus of the chapter is on selecting and preparing committed Black men to facilitate developmental group experiences, such as "The Young Lions" and "Black Manhood Training."

Role Model Presence in Black Communities: Tapping Black Male Resources

It is important that counselors initiate steps to acknowledge the importance of adult Black male influence on the development of Black boys. These steps must include a validation of such influence by incorporating it into the empowerment process. In most Black communities there is a wealth of positive Black male talent inherent in a variety of institutions and agencies that can be exploited in order to promote empowerment initiatives for young boys.

Churches. Contact the ministers of churches in Black communities and enlist their aid in recruiting concerned men from their congregations to serve as volunteers in the school. Most Black churches have organized men's groups, such as the ushers, or the deacon board, that may be willing to volunteer their services for empowerment efforts.

Community Agencies. Approach the directors of community recreation centers and other social service agencies for potential Black male volunteers. In many instances, such agencies have established youth programs that can serve as important supplements to school-based empowerment interventions.

Fraternities and Social/Service Organizations. In recent years, the graduate chapters of Black fraternities, as well as other social/service organizations in Black communities, have begun to actively address issues associated with young males. Contact these organizations to enlist a cadre of committed volunteers.

Black Businesses. Many Black businessmen have begun to express concern about the challenges facing young Black males. Contact Black entrepreneurs and seek their assistance as volunteers. Also, explore with them the possibility of establishing cooperative programs for Black male youth as a part of the empowerment process.

Colleges and Universities. Explore the possibility of recruiting male students from Black cultural and fraternal organizations on local college campuses. Discuss with academic officials at these institutions the possibility of volunteers receiving academic credit for their efforts.

Prior to venturing into the community, counselors may want to assess the possible Black male resources available in their own school settings. While a Black male presence is often limited in schools, it may be possible to recruit the talents of Black male teachers, administrators, and custodians into the empowerment efforts.

Regardless of the recruitment source, men considered as possible respected elders should, at minimum, exhibit the following criteria: 1) concern about the academic and social challenges facing Black male youth, 2) expressed commitment to helping young Black males, 3) insight into being Black and male, 4) demonstrated success in their personal endeavors, 5) a sense of responsibility, and 6) a willingness to grow as Black men.

From Concern to Action:
Preparing Black Men to be "Respected Elders"

Before assuming roles as respected elders, it is important that volunteers have the opportunity to increase their awareness, knowledge, and skills in several areas. First, they should have time to reflect on important aspects of Black manhood. Second, they should be provided with an overview of specific empowerment models for Black male youth. Third, they should learn basic information about group process and how to lead a group experience.

The following training program has been developed and used to prepare volunteers to work as respected elders with both "The Young Lions" and "Black Manhood Training" programs.

RESPECTED ELDERS TRAINING PROGRAM

Goal: To increase the awareness and promote the leadership skills of Black men who volunteer to conduct developmental group experiences with Black male youth in the school setting.

Training Schedule and Format:The training should be conducted in a minimum of sessions, ideally over a weekend to insure maximum participation. The training format consists of experiential group activities, lecture, and demonstration. This experience can be conducted in a variety of settings, including schools, churches, community centers, or private homes.

Number of Participants: The maximum number of participants for the training program is between 10 and 15.

SESSION 1: FRIDAY, 7-10 PM
Reflections on Black Manhood

This first session is devoted to having the participants take part in a group consciousness-raising experience. This experience is a modification of a developmental group program for Black men called "Reflections on the Native Son" (Lee, 1990). It is designed to help the participants raise their level of masculine consciousness. The experience aims to develop a supportive atmosphere that will enable the men to explore thoughts, feelings, and behaviors associated with being Black and male in contemporary American society.

A Black male facilitator is critical for this session. In addition, during this first session, women should be discouraged from either observing or participating in the process. This insures an atmosphere conducive to optimal male bonding and group discussion.

Methods of Facilitation:

1. "Images *of Black Men.*" Prepare a videotape presentation containing images of Black men. The short film *"Reflections of a Native Son"*, by Mustapha Khan (1989), excerpts from the film version of Richard Wright's *Native Son* (1986), excerpts from the Public Broadcasting System television version (1988) of Lorraine Hansberry's play, *A Raisin in the Sun*, and excerpts from the motion picture *"Glory"* (1990) are useful examples.

2. Divide the participants into small discussion groups and have them discuss their perceptions of the images of Black men in the videotape.

3. In the small groups have the participants discuss the following important questions to consider as Black men:

    • How do you see yourself as a Black man?
    • What is important to you as a Black man?

• How do you feel about all those negative stereotypes of and reports about Black men?, (e.g. Black men are shiftless, Black men treat Black women disrespectfully, Black men don't take fatherhood seriously, Black men are physically aggressive).

• How do you feel about the men in your family?

• What are your feelings about your own father?

• If you have children, what kind of a father would they say you are?

• If you have a son(s) how do you think he sees you as a father and as a man?

• When you were growing up, who were your heroes/role models?

• Who are your heroes/role models now?

• How do you feel about the women in your family?

• How do you see and what do you feel about women who are lovers/friends?

• What are the stresses and strains in your relationships with these women?

• What are the points of solid and deep agreement between you and women who are lovers/friends?

• What angers you, hurts you and brings you fulfillment in your relations with the significant women in your life?

• As a Black man, what brings you satisfaction?

• As a Black man, what gives you purpose?

• As a Black man, what role does religion play in your life?

• As a Black man, what makes you fearful?

• As a Black man, what makes you angry?

• At this point in your life, how do you feel about yourself as a Black man?

4. Bring all of the small groups back together and conduct a general discussion of new personal insights gained on Black manhood as result of the session.

5. Conduct a discussion of the concept of "Respected Elder."

SESSION 2: SATURDAY, 9 AM - 3 PM
Part I: 9 AM - 11 AM

Conduct an overview of empowerment model(s), e.g. *"The Young Lions"* or *"Black Manhood Training."*

Explain goals, methods of facilitation, and intended outcomes of model(s).

Part II: 11 AM - 1 PM

Provide participants with basic information on leading groups:

A. The group you lead will *not* be a therapy group. Therapeutic forces will be implicit in the group process, but this experience is *not* group therapy.

B. This will be a group guidance experience for young boys designed to give them an understanding of the Black man in history and culture, to develop in them the motivation and skill to achieve academically in school, to develop positive and responsible behavior among them, and to expose them to positive Black male role models.

C. The group will be a *structured* group - i.e., the discussion and focus of the group will follow a structured format.

D. As group leaders, your roles will include:
   • Initiator - suggesting ways to consider the topic under discussion

- Clarifier - making sure points, issues, etc. are clear to all group members
- Elaborator - expanding on points, ideas, and issues
- Coordinator - keeping order, clarifying relationships and pulling things together - *helping people to talk*
- Tester - making sure the group is on the same wavelength
- Summarizer - evaluating the group direction and reviewing the material covered

E. In addition, as group leader, you will perform the following tasks:

- Encouraging participation by all group members
- Mediating group conflicts
- Following group consensus on topics, ideas, etc.- *never overtly impose your will on the group*
- Gate-Tending - i.e., using both verbal and articulate members as well as reticent members for the good of the group process

F. Important Interpersonal Skills for Group Leaders
The goal for a group leader is to make each group member feel that he is an individual *and* a part of the group. The following are interpersonal skills for achieving this goal:

- Good non-verbal attending:
    - *S* - face members *squarely* during sessions
    - *O* - use an *open* posture
    - *L* - *lean* in toward members when talking
    - *E* - make appropriate *eye-contact*
    - *R* - appear *relaxed*
- Use of subtle encouragement- e.g., nodding head in the affirmative
- Respect for group members:

- don't interrupt members unnecessarily
- no value judgements, disapproval or shock
- value group members and try to understand them
- Genuineness — be for real
  - communicate without distracting messages
  - deal with what is going on in the "here and now"
  - be spontaneous and consistent
  - be willing to talk about yourself
- Empathy and Feelings
  - *empathy* is being able to "walk a mile in another brother's gym shoes"
  - in order to be empathic you have to be able to not only listen but to *hear* what another person is saying
  - by hearing what groups members are saying, they will hopefully deal with their feelings
  - in your group interactions, always go for the feelings, e.g. "How does that make you feel?"

    "How do the rest of you feel about that?"
    "You are feeling _____ because _____."

  - make sure that bad feelings are dealt with either in the group or individually
  - watch for body language, facial expressions, and voice tone for clues to uneasy feelings among group members
- Summarization - it is important to summarize at the beginning and end of each session
- Commitment and Confidentiality

Part III: 1 PM - 3 PM

Allow participants time to synthesize training, ask questions, and plan for program implementation.
- discuss personal perceptions of the *"Respected Elder"* concept
- work out the mechanics of program implementation in schools *e.g. selection of group participants, number of group sessions, scheduling of sessions, length of sessions, number of participants/group, initiation ceremony, program evaluation, and follow-up activities*
- questions and answers

FOLLOW-UP SESSION:
Conducted at the conclusion of
the Group Leadership Experience

After the men have completed their group leadership experience with the boys, a follow-up session should be conducted.
- allow the group leaders to analyze the entire experience
- discuss with the participants how being a *"respected elder"* has influenced their perceptions of themselves as Black men:

    1) What have you learned about being Black men as a result of this experience?

    2) As a result of your participation in this experience what specific changes do you think you will make as a Black man (academically, socially, within the community, etc.)?

3) What did you think about how the group was run? What is your opinion of specific activities? How would you change the group?

4) What was the most valuable part of the group for you personally?

5) Would you like to participate in another group such as this one?

TRAINING RESOURCES

Kahn, M. (1989). *Reflections of a native son.* [Film]. NY: Vanguard Films.

Wright, R. (1986). *Native son.* [Film]. Hollywood CA: Diane Silver Productions.

Hansberry, L. (1988). *A raisin in the sun* [Television Production]. Los Angeles, CA: NBLA Productions.

Glory (1990). [Film]. Hollywood CA: Tri-Star Pictures.

Corey, M.S. & Corey, G. (1992). *Groups: Process and practice. Fourth edition.* Pacific Grove, CA: Brooks/Cole.

Egan, G. (1990*). The skilled helper: A systematic approach to effective helping. 4th ed.* Pacific Grove, CA: Brooks/Cole.

REFERENCES

Lee, C. C. (1990). Black male development: "Counseling the Native Son." In F. Leafgren & D. Moore (Eds.), *Problem solving strategies and interventions for men in conflict* Alexandria, VA: AACD.

Patton, J. M. (1981). The Black male's struggle for an education. In L. E. Gary (Ed.), *Black men,* pp. 199-214. Beverly Hills, CA: Sage Press.

Washington, V., & Lee, C.C. (1982). Teaching and counseling Black males in grades K to 8. *Black Caucus: Journal of the National Association of Black Social Workers, 13,* 25-29.

CHAPTER SEVEN

EDUCATIONAL ADVOCACY FOR BLACK MALE STUDENTS

Anger, frustration, and, ultimately, failure represent the educational reality for scores of Black males. The disproportionate number of them who fail or become behaviorally labeled perpetuates a myth that they possess inherent educational deficiencies. Such thinking, however, obscures American educational reality. The educational difficulties confronting Black male youth are often not a function of deficient academic or social skills, but rather the outcome of structural factors. Traditionally, school success has generally been narrowly defined in terms of a White, middle-class female norm (Longstreth, 1974; Patton, 1981). Students whose realities differ from this norm are often required to make important adjustments to ensure a measure of success. If they are unable to do so, they are at considerable risk for mislabeling and negative tracking.

The preponderance of female educators, particularly at the elementary school level, has often created an environment that is not conducive to optimal learning for Black boys (Hale, 1982; Kunjufu, 1986; Patton, 1981; Washington & Lee, 1982.) According to Hale (1982), classrooms are generally oriented toward feminine values and the behaviors encouraged are those that are more natural for girls. While males of other ethnic backgrounds also experience problems in such an environment, Black males experience the greatest difficulty. This is especially the case when these educators have a limited understanding of or negative preconceived notions about the dynamics associated with Black male development, behavior, academic potential and culture. They see these boys as Black *and* male, therefore, they expect *"double trouble"* which can lead to a self-fulfilling prophesy (Washington & Lee, 1982).

In the majority of cases, the responsibility for problems in school comes to rest solely on the ethnic and gender status of the Black male student and his divergence from the educational norm. Little consideration is given to the notion that problematic functioning may in reality be reactive responses by Black male students to a system that tolerates little diversity.

The concerned counselor in such a setting is faced with a unique dilemma. Charged with facilitating Black male student adjustment to the educational system, he or she is confronted with the fact that it is often the system that needs adjustment to the Black male. This is particularly evident when the attitudes and practices of educators suggest a lack of sensitivity, to or understanding of, the dynamics associated with Black male development.

Role Definition: Counselors as Educational Advocates

The solution to this dilemma lies in a redefinition of the counseling role to account for the fact that problems are not always found in just Black male students; problems often exist in the educational system. Such a redefinition requires an awareness of the systemic barriers to quality education faced by young Black males and the development of strategies to effectively challenge them.

The role of *educational advocate* represents such redefinition. The concerned counselor, in such a role, can initiate consultation activities to help his or her fellow educators better understand the dynamics of male development from a Black perspective and make the teaching-learning process more relevant to the realities of young Black males.

A major consultation activity for educational advocates is described in this chapter. It is a seminar for educators that counselors might consider coordinating with a mandate from school district officials. It has been developed as a comprehensive inservice training experience for teachers and other school personnel on understanding Black male development and promoting academic success among young Black boys.

Background

The seminar is designed as a seven-week training experience. Each session is scheduled for approximately three hours. Consideration should be given to the possibility of conducting this seminar as an after school (e.g., 4 PM to 7 PM) professional development activity or as a summer training institute. Plans should be made to award Continuing Education Units, Recertification Points, or College Credit to participants for completing such a seminar.

The teaching of this seminar may need to be a collaborative effort among a school system, local colleges and universities, and community resources. Experts in areas such as Black child and adolescent development, Black psychology, African/ African-American history and culture, men's issues, multicultural counseling, and curriculum development should be invited to contribute their expertise to the seminar.

Counselors should be prepared to justify to teachers, administrators, school district officials, and the community-at-large the rationale for developing an in-service experience that focuses exclusively on the educational needs of one student group. An important argument for conducting such an experience lies in the data which present the profile of Black males as most at-risk in most school systems. One way to prevent the academic and social problems confronting this group is to help teachers and other educators develop the awareness, knowledge, and skills to better promote Black male learning.

While the seminar should be open to all educators, it is highly recommended for teachers of grades 3-4. As noted previously, these have been found to be particularly problematic years in the educational development of Black males.

PROFESSIONAL DEVELOPMENT SEMINAR: ISSUES IN EDUCATING BLACK MALES

SEMINAR DESCRIPTION:

This seminar provides an overview of the issues and challenges related to the educational development of young Black males in contemporary schools. Emphasis will be placed on strategies for promoting the academic success of Black males. Participants will also gain an appreciation of African/ African-American culture and its role in promoting the psychosocial development of male youth.

Objectives

1) To raise educator awareness of personal values and biases which may be detrimental to the welfare of Black male students.

2) To increase educator awareness of the developmental issues and challenges facing Black males.

3) To provide historical/statistical/cultural information to elevate educator awareness of the challenges confronting Black males.

4) To identify instructional practices which impede academic progress for Black males.

5) To identify instructional practices which enhance academic progress for Black males.

SEMINAR CONTENT:

Session 1: Introduction and Overview

- Seminar Introduction - Review of Goals, Objectives, Readings, Requirements, etc.
- The Black Male in America: A Social/Historical

Overview
- Education and Achievement of Young Black Males:
  A National and Local Overview
- "Fourth Grade Failure Syndrome"

Session 2: Examining Educator Attitudes and Behavior
- Experiential Activity 1: Exploring Personal Attitudes
Toward Black Males
Divide seminar participants into small groups. Have them
take a few minutes to reflect upon the following questions and
then discuss their answers in the small groups.

- To what extent do you regularly interact with Black
  males? Professionally? Socially?

- What was your parents' main advice to you
  about Black males?

- How would your parents have responded if, while
  in college, you had invited a Black male home
  with you for Thanksgiving?

- How would you respond if your teenage
  daughter was dating a Black male?

- How do you think you would respond if your
  college-age daughter announced plans to marry a
  Black male?

- What is the origin or source of most of your
  views about Black males? What have you ever done
  to validate your beliefs about Black males? How
  do your beliefs affect your behavior toward Black
  males in the classroom?

- What is the nicest/meanest, most helpful/hurtful
  thing a Black male ever said or did to you? What
  did you feel? What did you do?

- Describe how you feel when you teach or think
  about teaching young Black males.

- What personal attributes do you have which enhance your working with Black males in the class room?
• Debriefing

• Experiential Activity 2: Examining Classroom Behavior Toward Black Males

Have seminar participants examine incidences of discipline in their classrooms and answer the following:

- Do the Black males in my class receive a disproportionate share of reprimands or negative feedback?

Have participants examine other classroom behaviors and answer the following:

- Do the stereotypes or perceptions I may have acquired about Black boys influence my behavior towards them and expectations of them?
- Do I expect disciplinary problems from them and behave accordingly?
- Do I expect low achievement from them and behave accordingly?
- Is my instructional behavior reactive, rather than proactive when it comes to Black males?
• Debriefing

Session 3: Psychosocial Development
• The Psychosocial Development of Black Males: The Childhood and Adolescent Years

Session 4: African/African-American Male Culture
• *"Cool Pose"* as a Cultural Signature of Young Black Males: Exploring Positive Black Male Attitudes, Values, and Behaviors and their Cultural Origins

Session 5: Cognitive Styles: Implications for the Effective
Teaching of Black Males
- Definition of Cognitive Style
- Cognitive Style and Cultural Groupings
- Cognitive Style Comparisons
- Cognitive Style Implications for the Teaching of Black
  Males

Session 6: Curriculum Content and Methods That Enhance
Academic Progress for Black Male Students

- Integrating the Accomplishments of Black Men into the
  Existing Curriculum
- Examining Curriculum to Insure that Black Males
  are Included in Primary and Non-stereotyped Roles.
- Insuring the Inclusion of Black Males in Classroom
  Activities (e.g., tutors, educational assistants,
  storytellers, "room fathers," and field-trip escorts)
- Encouraging the Participation of Black Males in Parent-
  Teacher Associations and Other SchoolOrganizations
- The Importance of Non-educational Personnel (e.g. Black
  male custodians and lunchroom staff) as Valid Role
  Models/Mentors

Session 7: FORUM—Perspectives on the Education of Young
Black Males
A panel of Black men from various social and professional
backgrounds will discuss their personal educational experiences
and offer their perceptions of the current state of education for
young Black males.

SEMINAR READINGS

Required Texts:

Gibbs, J. T. (Ed.). (1988). *Young, Black, and male in America: An endangered species*. New York: Auburn House.

Hale, J. (1982). *Black children, their roots, culture, and learning styles*. Provo, UT: Brigham Young University Press.

Majors, R., & Bilson, J. M. (1993). *Cool pose: The dilemmas of Black manhood in America*. New York: Simon & Schuster.

Required Readings:

Anderson, J. A. (1988). Cognitive styles and multicultural populations. *Journal of Teacher Education, 39,* 2-9.

Boykins, W. (1983). The academic performance of Afro-American children. In J. Spence (Ed.), *Achievement and achievement motives* (pp. 321-371). San Francisco, CA: W. H. Freeman Co.

Cazanave, N. (1981). Black men in America: The quest for manhood. In H. McAdoo (Ed.), *Black families*. Beverly Hills (pp. 176-185). CA: Sage Publications.

Gaston, J. (1986). The destruction of the young Black male: The impact of popular culture and organized sports. *Journal of Black Studies, 16,* 36

Kunjufu, J. (1985). *Countering the conspiracy to destroy Black boys*. Chicago, IL: African American Images.

Kunjufu, J. (1986). *Countering the conspiracy to destroy Black boys* (Vol.2) Chicago, IL: African American Images.

Patton, J. (1981). The Black males's struggle for an education. In L.E. Gary (Ed.), *Black men* (pp. 191-214). Beverly Hills, CA: Sage Publications.

Staples, R. (1978). Masculinity and race: The dual dilemma of Black men. *Journal of Social Issues, .34,* 169-183.

Taylor, R. L. (1989). Black youth, role models, and the social construction of identity. In R. L. Jones (Ed.), *Black adolescents*. Berkeley, CA: Cobb & Henry Publishers.

Washington, V., & Lee, C. C. (1982). Teaching and counseling Black males in grades K to 8. *Journal of the National Association of Black Social Workers, 13*, 25-29

SUGGESTED READINGS:

Brown, C. (1965). *Manchild in the promised land.* New York: Macmillan.

Haley, A. & X, M. (1964). *The autobiography of Malcom X.* New York: Grove Press, Inc.

Wright, R. (1937). *Black boy.* New York: Harper & Row.

Wright, R. (1940). *Native son.* New York: Harper & Row.

SEMINAR REQUIREMENTS

1. Readings: Required texts and readings.
2. Participation: Small group activities and seminar discussion will be an important part of the instruction.
3. Written Assignments: Four, 300 word essays reacting to any of the required readings. The essays must include the following points:
    a) a brief summary of the author's main points or ideas
    b) your reactions, questions, opinions, etc. regarding the author's ideas from your vantage point as a teacher or possible teacher of young Black males.
4. Lesson Plan: A fully developed lesson plan (Goals, Behavioral Objectives, Methods, Materials and Resources, and Evaluation) in a specific content area that incorporates Black male accomplishments and makes allowances for Black male learning styles.

CONCLUSION

A seminar such as this demonstrates a commitment on the part of a school system to foster maximum educational development for Black males. Counselors, acting as educational advocates, can be in the forefront of initiating such a consultation activity. They can help their fellow educators better understand the dynamics of male development from a Black perspective and make the teaching-learning process more relevant to the realities of young Black males.

REFERENCES

Hale, J. (1982). *Black children, their roots, culture, and learning styles.* Provo, UT: Brigham Young University Press.

Kunjufu, J. (1985). *Countering the conspiracy to destroy Black boys.* Chicago, IL: African American Images.

Longstreth, L. E. (1974). *Psychological development of the child (2nd ed.)* New York: New York Press.

Patton, J. M. (1981). The Black male's struggle for an education. In L.E. Gary (Ed.) *Black men.* (pp. 191-214). Beverly Hills, CA: Sage Publications.

Washington, V., & Lee, C.C. (1982). Teaching and counseling Black males in grades K to 8. *Journal of the National Association of Black Social Workers, 13,* 25-29.

CHAPTER 8

" S.O.N.S." :
EMPOWERMENT STRATEGIES FOR AFRICAN AMERICAN PARENTS

MS. JONES

Several years ago, I did a presentation on empowering young Black males at a conference in Richmond, Virginia. At the end of my presentation, a Black woman (I will call her Ms. Jones) came up to me with concerns about her own son. Ms. Jones was a school counselor who had been divorced for several years. As a result of the divorce, she was raising a son by herself. She said that although it had been a struggle raising her son alone while he was in elementary school, the challenges had become more pronounced now that he was in middle school. She expressed to me that being a single parent of an adolescent boy was becoming overwhelming. He increasingly refused to listen, shirked responsibilities at home, and withdrew from most interactions with her. While a good student in elementary school, his grades had begun to slip significantly. She was afraid that if things continued the way they were, she would lose her son to the streets and he would become a negative

statistic, like so many other Black male youth. Being both mother *and* father to her son was becoming an increasing source of frustration and stress for her. Although she wished her son could have more contact with his father or some other male parental figure, she did not see this as being a very realistic possibility. She implored me, *"Please, Dr. Lee I need your help. How does a single Black woman raise a healthy son?"*

Ms. Jones' anxiety and frustration concerning her son are typical of the feelings experienced by many contemporary African American mothers. Data suggest that parenthood among African Americans can often be a complicated issue. According to The Urban League, Black, female-headed families embraced 50% of all Black families with children in 1985 (Watson & Johnson 1990). Significantly, in low-income urban areas, Black families headed by single teenage mothers comprise the fastest growing category of family groups (Lewis, 1992). The Urban League report goes on to state that in the course of their childhood, 86% of Black children are likely to spend some time in a single-parent household, more than twice the rate for White children (Watson & Johnson 1990).

Parents represent the first and most important socializing agent for the young. The active participation of parents is crucial if young children are to master the most fundamental of human developmental tasks (Erikson, 1950; Piaget, 1970). If this is to be achieved, however, parents must provide for, protect, and nurture their children. Parenthood, therefore, is characterized by a total dedication to a myriad of complex, and often challenging, tasks aimed at providing optimal conditions for the healthy psychosocial development of children.

It is apparent that scores of African American women must confront the complicated tasks of parenthood alone. In many instances, they must single-handedly foster the development of their children in environments characterized by alienation, drugs, violence, and unemployment (Dash, 1989; Edelman, 1988; McAdoo, 1981; Ogbu, 1988; Winters, 1993). Their dedication to parenthood can often be severely taxed as they struggle to provide for basic family needs. Their challenge is how to raise children who are psychologically and socially sound, despite the negative environmental forces that often impinging upon family life.

Because academic and social empowerment for young Black males is predicated, in large measure, on guidance and reinforcement from parents, this chapter presents a workshop to help Black parents acquire the knowledge and skills necessary for promoting the development of their sons. The philosophical foundation for the workshop draws from the historical strength of Black families. It also draws from empirical evidence which suggests that enlightened parent involvement can significantly influence the academic and social development of young people. Such enlightenment can be gained from educational programs which have emerged that offer parents new information about what can be done to put their children at a psychosocial advantage in society.

Given the statistics presented in the first paragraph, this chapter focuses on strategies that Black mothers, particularly those who find themselves raising sons without the benefit of a male parent-figure, can employ to empower their sons. While the concepts and strategies presented in the workshop have relevance for empowering daughters as well, the focus of the intervention is on male youth. The data presented earlier in this book on the societal challenges facing Black males underscore the importance of focusing on strategies for raising healthy, stress-resistant sons.

This workshop is designed to complement those programs for Black male youth presented in chapters four and five. Prior to a discussion of the workshop, a brief overview of its philosophical foundation is provided.

The Strength of the Black Family

Initiatives to assist Black parents in empowering male youth must be based on an appreciation of the historical strength of the African American family. Such an appreciation is critical given the generally pathological view of Black family life presented in much of the social-science literature (Moynihan, 1965; Rainwater, 1970). In general, this view suggests that because of poverty, the African American family unit is characteristically disorganized, resulting in cognitive, affective, and behavioral deficits in children. Research to support this view implies that if African American parents adopt the norms and values of European-American, middle-class families, they will promote the successful psychosocial development of their children.

Over the years, however, African American scholars have presented an alternative view that disputes pathological notions of Black family life. This view establishes a legacy of continuity, hard-work, kinship, love, pride, respect, and stability in the evolution of Black families in America (Billingsley, 1968, 1992; Frazier, 1939; Hill, 1972; McAdoo, 1988; Martin & Martin, 1980; Staples, 1974). This, despite the history of discrimination, racism, oppression, and poverty which has characterized much of the African American experience. In the face of extreme environmental hardship, scores of African American families have found the inner resources to effectively cope; have promoted the positive development of children; and have ultimately prevailed across generations.

Hayles (1991), in reviewing the research literature on effective family functioning among African Americans, summarized the following empirically documented strengths of African American families:

- *Kinship networks and extended family systems*
- *Value systems that emphasize such things as harmony, cooperation, interdependence, acceptance of difference/diversity, internal development, strong work and achievement orientation, and traditionalism*
- *Strong male/female bonds*
- *Role adaptability and flexibility*
- *Roots, emotional support and buffers or consolations against racism*
- *Respect, appreciation and full utilization of the skills and wisdom of senior family members*
- *Child centeredness*

Importantly, these family strengths appear to have a direct link to the African cultural heritage of African Americans. There is significant scholarly discussion concerning an important cultural continuity between African and African American family life (McAdoo, 1981; Nobles, 1974; Sudarkasa, 1980, 1981). Analysis and interpretation of family patterns among Black people in both Africa and the United States suggest that African American family organization evolved from the patterns recreated by enslaved Africans brought to this country in the seventeenth century (Genovese, 1974; Gutman, 1976; Sudarkasa, 1980).

The family value system inherent in these strengths is characteristically evident despite variations in African American family structure. Whether one considers a nuclear family with a husband, wife, and children, a nuclear family with a single parent and children, or an extended family with parents, children, and other relatives present, these optimal dimensions of family functioning are evident among African American families across the social and economic spectrum (Billingsley, 1968).

Promoting family involvement in Black male empowerment should be approached with the understanding that this institution is a strong and viable force for enhancing psychosocial development.

Parent Involvement/Education: A Crucial Key to Youth Empowerment

Informed parent involvement in the lives of children and adolescents significantly influences these young people's psychosocial development. Operationally defined, parent involvement includes all activities in which parents are actively engaged in support of their children. These activities include formal and informal programs and individual or group actions at any level of parent participation (Warnat, 1980). The quality of parental involvement is often enhanced through parent education. Parent education can be considered any formal attempt to increase parents' knowledge of, and facility with, skills associated with raising children (Lamb & Lamb, 1978).

Concern over raising children properly, as well as providing education to parents to help insure that they do so, has a long history in the United States (Warnat, 1980). Significantly, within the last fifty years interest has centered on educating parents so that they develop a firm, consistent, democratic, and loving approach in handling children. Parents have also been advised to adjust their parenting approaches to match a child's developmental stage. In addition, research has stressed the importance of the father's role as an active participant in child-rearing (Warnat, 1980).

Within the context of these views on parenthood, formal parent education programs have recently emerged that teach parents what they need to know and do to promote the academic and social development of their children (Goins, 1993; Alvy, 1985). While these initiatives vary in terms of training focus, their primary goal is to help parents use their inherent family strengths and resources more effectively to enhance the development of their children. Specific objectives include helping parents develop skills involved with child management, child-rearing, parent-child communication, and general care of the child.

Research suggests that parent education programs are generally beneficial for both parents and children. Data on the impact of such programs suggest that they can significantly improve various aspects of family relationships including, positive parental control of child behavior, increased family cohesion, effective parent-child communication, and decreased family conflict (Giannotti & Doyle, 1982; Hammond & Schutz, 1980; Noller & Taylor, 1989; Pinsker & Geoffrey, 1981).

A crucial aspect of parent education initiatives is promoting involvement in children's education. Many parent education programs stress the need for parents to play an active role in all aspects of their children's school experience. Again, research would suggest that improvement in academic performance on the part of children is directly related to the degree to which parents are involved in their children's formal education (Comer, 1986; Henderson, 1987; Lewis, 1992).

Parent Involvement/Education: An African American Perspective

While there are universal aspects to parenthood, it is important to note that significant cultural differences exist in the nature of parenting patterns and techniques. These are associated with important cultural values that form notions of parenthood. This is particularly important to consider when viewing parent involvement and education from an African American perspective.

Being an African American parent is a phenomenon that can be complicated simply by the differences in cultural values and traditions, discussed previously, that are often contradictory to the contemporary European-American, middle-class culture and value system (Hill, 1992). In addition, economic and social challenges can place considerable stress on African American parents, often stifling their effectiveness and involvement with their children.

Given the cultural and socioeconomic factors that shape the parenting techniques of African Americans, attempts have been made to develop new culture-specific parenting paradigms as well as adapt existing parenting programs to meet the needs of African American parents (Comer & Poussaint, 1975; Hale-Benson, 1986; Harrison & Alvy, 1982; Hill, 1992; Hopson & Hopson, 1990). A major focus of these paradigms and programs involves helping African American parents develop skills to foster a positive racial identity in their children. This is of critical importance since American society has historically done little to foster a sense of pride in Blackness among African American children. Significantly, a strong racial identity has been found to have a direct link to academic and social success for African American children (Banks & Grambs, 1972; Clark, 1983;).

A primary emphasis in Black parent education and involvement is on promoting attitudes and skills among children that will enable them to cope effectively with social and economic forces; forces that often damage self-esteem and diminish a sense of control over the environment. Significantly, research on culture-specific parent education and involvement initiatives suggests that when African American parents feel that they have a greater impact on their children's lives, significant academic and social gains generally ensue (Slaughter & Kuehne, 1988; McQueen & Washington, 1988; Winters, 1993).

Background for the Workshop

In recent years, attempts have been made to adapt existing parenting programs to meet the needs of African American parents and families. These efforts have resulted in new initiatives aimed at empowering African American parents by providing them information and skills on parenting and by detailing the commitments necessary to strengthen Black families (Alvy, 1985; Comer & Poussaint, 1975; Hill, 1992; Hopson & Hopson, 1990).

These initiatives provide a culture-specific guide for parenting that promotes the African/African-American cultural legacy found in the Black family which serves as the foundation for strong families (Hill, 1992). Within this context, Alvy (1985) offers a rationale for participation by African American parents in parenting programs by identifying five life goals for Black children: *1) loving relationships, 2) good jobs, 3) good education, 4) helping the Black community, and 5) resisting the pressure of the street.*

Given these goals, culture-specific parenting programs address a number of issues considered important for African American parents, including: *1) parenting in White America, 2) the history and legacy of the African American family, 3) cultural awareness, 4) effective parent-child communication, 5) school success, 6) the developmental stages of childhood, 7) discipline and self-esteem, and 8) health and spirituality.*

The workshop described here builds on previous African American parenting program initiatives. It is an educational experience that is designed to help African American parents, particularly mothers, enhance skills to promote the academic and social development of male children.

The workshop is called "S.O.N.S." (Strengthen Our Native Sons). It is designed to be a short-term educational experience for African American parents which enhances the knowledge and skills necessary for promoting the academic and social development of male youth. While the workshop has been conceived as an experience for both mothers and fathers, it primarily focuses on providing support to mothers, in particular those mothers who are raising sons without the benefit of a male partner.

As previously mentioned, the workshop was developed to be an adjunct to the *"Young Lions"* and *"Black Manhood Training,"* the empowerment programs described in chapters four and five. Parents might be invited to attend this workshop while their sons are participating in programs such as the *"Young Lions"* or *"Black Manhood Training."*

The success of this workshop is predicated on the principles of flexibility and informality. In planning the experience, careful consideration should be given to the time constraints facing many parents. Therefore, workshop sessions should be scheduled during evening hours, over weekends, or at other times that will not conflict with work or child-care schedules.

Workshop sessions should be conducted in an atmosphere that emphasizes comfort. Thought should be given to conducting the workshop in homes or community centers. (e.g. churches or community social or recreational centers). Efforts should be made to make the workshop setting as informal and inviting as possible. Parents should perceive the workshop as a supportive setting where they can freely express feelings associated with raising a son. Whenever necessary, arrangements should be made for child-care, so as to encourage participation in the workshop.

The workshop has been designed to be run by a professional counselor as a consultation initiative. However, anyone with knowledge of African/African-American culture, child and adolescent development, or parent education may participate in workshop facilitation. Importantly, parents who have completed the workshop might be considered as co-facilitators for succeeding experiences.

It is important that the facilitator adopt an adult-learner approach for the workshop. He or she should communicate to participants that the real knowledge about raising a son rests with them and that the workshop will be a forum for the sharing of their collective wisdom. Therefore, optimal learning will occur when participants share their experiences with the group. The facilitator should impress upon the participants that their experience as parents means that they have much to contribute to the workshop.

The workshop is presented here as an eight session educational experience. However, the length of the workshop may be modified to make allowances for the demands on parents' time. The general framework of the workshop is for the participants to meet in sessions that consist of lecturettes, experiential activities, and group discussions concerning parenting issues. Sessions should be scheduled to last for approximately 2 hours.

"S.O.N.S."
(STRENGTHEN OUR NATIVE SONS)

Purpose: To incorporate family resources into the Black male empowerment process by helping parents, particularly mothers, acquire and enhance skills that will promote the psychosocial development of their sons.

Goals:
1) To help parents gain a better understanding of the roles and functions of parenthood.
2) To help parents consider parenthood from an Afrocentric perspective.
3) To help parents acquire and enhance skills for effective discipline.
4) To help parents acquire and enhance skills for effective parent-child communication.
5) To help parents achieve a better understanding of Black male physical growth and psychosocial development in childhood and adolescence.

6) To help parents acquire and enhance skills for promoting self-esteem and a positive cultural identity in sons.

7) To help parents acquire and enhance skills for promoting a sense of responsibility in their sons.

8) To help parents acquire and enhance skills for promoting school success among their sons.

9) To provide parents with a supportive atmosphere to explore the challenges, issues, and feelings associated with raising an African American male child in contemporary society.

Session 1   *The Nature of Parenthood*

Goal: To examine the roles and function of parenthood and to have participants begin to reflect on the challenges and opportunities associated with raising a Black male child in contemporary society.

Methods of Facilitation

1) Conduct an exercise that allows the participants to introduce themselves. For example, have each participant remove three things of value from his or her wallet or purse. Invite each participant to explain the valued items to the group. Facilitate a discussion of the possible commonalities found among these items.

2) Review the purpose and goals of the workshop. Explain to the participants that the workshop will be both informal and informational. Suggest that the experience will provide them with the opportunity to learn new ideas about being a parent and to share their issues and concerns about raising a son with the other participants. Stress the notion of the adult-learner model.

3) Begin a discussion of the purpose of parenthood (e.g.,

provide for, protect, teach, nurture, set limits, etc.) and the major roles (e.g. teacher, role model, enforcer, etc.) that parents should assume. List purposes and roles on chalkboard or newsprint.

4) Invite each participant to "tell his/her story," i.e., have him/her tell the group about his/her son (s) and any parenting issues or concerns they have. List commonalities in issues and concerns on chalkboard or newsprint.

5) Have the participants review the list of issues and concerns and ask, "How many of these issues are linked to the challenges facing Black males in society today?"

6) Invite the participants to share hopes and aspirations for their sons.

7) Invite the participants to respond to the following questions: "When it comes to raising my son, what things do I do well?" "What things could I do better in raising my son?" List responses on news print or chalkboard.

8) As a final activity have the participants share telephone numbers and addresses so that they can maintain contact between sessions. Encourage them to contact each other for support and advice when confronted with parenting challenges.

Session 2   *Parenting: An Afrocentric Perspective*

Goal: To have participants reflect on the history and legacy of the African/African-American family and to develop a parenting perspective that emphasizes Afrocentric cultural traditions.

Methods of Facilitation

1) Summarize the strengths of African American

families outlined by Hayles (1991). Invite the participants to reflect on the cultural legacy and strength, as well as parenting patterns, within their family of origin with the following questions:

1. What generation in the United States do you think you represent?

2. What social conditions or conflicts did your ancestors experience within the United States? What migration experiences did your ancestors have?

3. Did grandparents or other relatives live with you when you were growing up?

4. Did you live with both of your parents?

5. What kind of work did your parents do?

6. Did your father do what would be considered "women's work" in the home? Did your mother do what would be considered "men's work?"

7. How many brothers and sisters do you have? Are you the oldest, youngest, middle child? Did older children take care of younger children when you were growing up?

8. Were your parents strict or lenient in the way they dealt with you when you were growing up?

9. Did your parents have family rules? What were some of these rules?

10. Are there any values your parents taught you? e.g. "always do your best", "respect other people," etc.?

11. Did you have chores to do at home? What were these chores? How often did you have to do them?

12. Did you talk to your parents about

problems you had, or private things that were important to you (things you did not talk about with just anybody)?

13. What did your parents tell you about school and getting an education?
14. Was your family religious? Did your family go to church? How often?
15. What did your parents tell you about the value of work?
16. Was there a concern about African American political, social, or cultural activities in your family?
17. How did your family confront and deal with problems or crises?

2) From these family reflections have the participants consider commonalities that point to the strength of African American families. List on chalkboard or newsprint. Ask, "How do these early family influences affect your parenting today?"

3) Conduct a discussion of the following question, "How do the challenges facing you as a parent differ from those that confronted your parents when they were raising you?"

4) Introduce the concept of *Afrocentrism:* 1) A philosophy that places Africa at the center of one's view of the world, 2) A philosophy that emphasizes devoting energies to uplifting Black people, 3) A philosophy that emphasizes the adoption of images, symbols, lifestyles, and manners that reflect the positive aspects of African culture(Asante,1988).Suggest that Afrocentric principles should be incorporated into strategies for raising a healthy Black male child.

5) Introduce the seven principles of *Nguzu Saba,* developed by Dr. Malana Ron Karenga in 1965:

- *Umoja (Unity).* To strive for and maintain unity in the family, community, nation, and race.
- *Kujichagulia (Self-determination).* To define our selves, name ourselves, create for ourselves, and speak for ourselves instead of being defined, named created for, and spoken for, by others.
- *Ujima (Collective Work and Responsibility).* To build and maintain our community together and make our sisters' and brothers' problems our problems, and to solve them together.
- *Ujamaa (Cooperative Economics).* To build and maintain our own stores, shops, and other businesses and to profit from them together.
- *Nia (Purpose).* To make our collective vocation the building, and developing, of our community in order to restore our people to their traditional greatness.
- *Kuumba (Creativity).* To do always as much as we can, in order to leave our community more beautiful and better off than when we inherited it.
- *Imani (Faith).* To believe with all our heart in our people, our parents, our teachers, our leaders, and the righteousness and victory of our struggle.

These Afrocentric principles lay the foundation for an African American world view that promotes the individual, the family, and the community. Stress the idea that positive African American family life should be centered around these principles. Discuss with the participants why it would be important to raise a son employing these principles.

6) Provide participants with the following:

Guidelines for Raising a Son - An Afrocentric Perspective

- Teach your son about his family history.

Emphasize the strengths, values, and traditions established and perpetuated in your family.

• Observe holidays *(e.g. Kwanzaa, "Juneteenth")* and family gatherings as a way to teach your son about culture and traditions.

• Have your son participate in periodic family gatherings and activities.

• Familiarize your son with African/African-American cultural rituals.

• Provide your son with *"Rites of Passage"* experiences to celebrate his life transitions (See Chapter 5).

• Teach your son roles and responsibilities that will contribute to the overall development of the family.

• Help your son to develop academic, career, and personal-social goals and objectives that will bring honor to self and family.

• Help your son develop a sense of service to the African American community.

• Provide spiritual education to your son as a basis for personal and family values.

Facilitate a discussion about these guidelines and possible parenting strategies for implementing them.

Session 3 *Fostering Self-Esteem and Pride in Blackness*

Goal: To have participants explore methods which promote self-esteem and foster a positive cultural identity in their sons.

Methods of Facilitation:

1) Provide participants with a brief definition of self-esteem: *How people feel about themselves.* Discuss with participants how children develop a sense of self-esteem. Stress the significant impact that

parents and teachers can have on children's
self-esteem.

2) Consider the educational and social challenges that
   may stifle high self-esteem among Black male youth.
   Ask: "What people, things, events, or
   situations would keep your son from feeling good
   about himself as a young Black male?"

3) Provide the participants with a definition of "Black
   Pride": A positive attitude, love, and respect
   for Black people and their heritage and culture.

4) Present to, and discuss with, the participants the
   following:

Guidelines for Promoting Self Esteem and Black Pride in Your Son

- Express satisfaction with your son's abilities
  and characteristics.
- Provide verbal (e.g. praise) and physical (e.g. hugs)
  appreciation for all of your son's efforts and achievements.
- Avoid disparaging remarks about African Americans,
  particularly African American males.
- Insure that African/African-American images
  are displayed in the home (e.g. artwork, family
  photographs, periodicals, etc.).
- Start and continuously expand on a home library containing
  books, audiotapes, videotapes, and other materials
  that chronicle African and African-American heritage and
  the achievements of Africans and African Americans
  (particularly males) for your son. Spend "quality time"
  exploring and discussing these media with your son.
- Encourage family celebrations and commemorations
  of African American holidays (e.g. Kwanzaa,
  Martin Luther King's Birthday, Black History
  Month, "Juneteenth").

- Visit African/African-American cultural institutions with your son (e.g. museums, historical monuments/shrines, art galleries, cultural festivals, etc.).
- Encourage older male family members to share stories of their youth with your son.
- Talk openly and frankly with your son about the issue of racism and the challenges which confront Black males in American society. Help him to develop strategies to deal effectively with this issue and its accompanying societal challenges.

    5) ACTION PLANNING: Encourage the participants to assist each other in developing personal action plans that will contain strategies to enhance their parenting efforts. Inform them that this plan will continue to grow as they move through the workshop. Have them brainstorm individual strategies that will promote self esteem and a sense of Black pride in their sons.

Session 4   *Understanding Your Son: An "Owners Manual" for Parents*

Goal: To give the participants important information for a better understanding of the physical growth and psychosocial development of Black male youth. Ideas on how parents can promote this growth and development will be offered.

Methods of Facilitation:

    1) Have the participants share stories about issues and challenges they have confronted in their attempts to understand and promote the physical growth and psychosocial development of their sons.

    2) Provide the participants with specific information on the physical, cognitive, language, moral, and social developmental milestones of childhood and adolescence. Discuss with them the physical

and emotional milestones of infancy, early childhood, middle childhood, and puberty and adolescence.

3) Conduct an exploration and discussion of the unique developmental tasks and issues of childhood and adolescence that relate to being Black and male in America as delineated by Crawley and Freeman (1993). These specific tasks and issues are discussed in chapter two. Stress the importance of implementing the personal action plans, discussed previously, that promote self esteem and Black pride in their sons. Such plans would help their son master these race-and gender-specific developmental tasks.

4) Conduct a discussion of the relationship between health habits and positive physical and psychosocial development. Introduce the concept that the care and nurturance of sons are predicated on the following conditions:
   - A nutritious and well-balanced diet.
   - Healthy, sanitary, and stable living conditions.
   - Opportunities for family rest, relaxation, and exercise.
   - Preventive health care, e.g., regular physical examinations and dental care.

Encourage the participants to share ideas on ways to foster such conditions. Participants should be encouraged to add strategies for promoting these conditions to their personal action plans.

Session 5 *Effective Discipline*

Goal: To assist participants in refining behavior management skills and exploring ways to promote self-discipline in their sons.

Methods of Facilitation:

1) Facilitate a discussion of the greatest discipline or behavior management challenges confronted by the participants. List these on newsprint or chalkboard. Examine differences and commonalities among the challenges.

2) Have the participants develop and role play a series of situations involving discipline or behavior management issues they have encountered with their sons. Have participants take turns playing parent and son in these situations. Using these role plays, help the participants formulate strategies for dealing effectively with the discipline issues presented.

3) Provide the participants with the following:
   Guidelines for Promoting Discipline
   • Remember that discipline should be an expression of love and care.
   • Approach the issue of discipline with the attitude, "I am the parent, you are the child."
   • Model the behavior you want from your son.
   • Communicate and explain your rules to your son.
   • Allow your son to comment upon, but not determine, the rules in your household.
   • Establish consequences for the infraction of rules.
   • Be consistent and follow through on the consequences when rules are broken.
   • Give reinforcement and praise for appropriate behavior when your son does the right thing.
   • Show your son love and sincerity.

4) Introduce the notion that the ultimate goal of behavior management is to enable a boy to develop self-discipline, or the ability to control his own thoughts, feelings, and behavior in order to achieve positive life outcomes. Ask the participants to consider the following question:

"Given the challenges that threaten the well-being of Black males in contemporary society (e.g. drugs, violence, etc.), why is it so important that your sons develop self-discipline?"

5) Provide the participants with the following: Guidelines for Promoting Self-Discipline
   • Teach your son the importance of delayed gratification.
   • Teach your son how to control anger and aggression.
   • Teach your son to be respectful and considerate of others.
   • Teach your son the importance of developing spiritual values as the basis for a personal sense of morality
   • Teach your son to resist the pressures of the "street" and the lure of illegal activities.

6) Encourage participants to help each other develop specific, proactive strategies in their personal action plans for enhancing behavior management and for teaching self-discipline.

Session 6   *Developing Responsibility*

Goal: To assist participants in promoting a sense of responsibility in their sons.

Methods of Facilitation:

1) Have participants list and discuss the chores and other duties their sons are responsible for in the home and community.

2) Provide participants with the following: Guidelines for Promoting Responsibility
   • Teach your son that, ultimately, he is responsible for his behavior and its consequences.
   • Ensure that your son has a specified set of duties

that make a significant contribution to the running of your household. Develop penalties for failure to carry out these duties.

- Encourage your son to seek gainful age - appropriate employment outside of the home (e.g. running errands for neighbors, delivering newspapers, cutting grass, baby-sitting, working at a fast-food restaurant, etc.)
- Encourage your son to become active in community organizations, particularly those that advance African American empowerment.

3) Conduct a discussion with the participants about the importance of allowing their sons to grow gradually into manhood. Stress the importance of not placing responsibilities on boys that they are not ready to handle. As an example, consider the expectation often placed on young boys that they act as, *"the man of the house"* in the absence of an adult male. Ask the participants to consider the following questions:

Is this an appropriate expectation? What kind of burden does such an expectation place upon a young boy? What happens to the parent-child relationship when a boy is placed in the "man of the house" role?

Given the fact that in many cases, a male child is the only "man" in the house, what are some age-appropriate ways that he can be called upon to assist in the household?

4) Introduce the importance of helping sons develop responsible sexual behavior. Share with the participants data about the sex-related challenges that disproportionately confront African Americans (e.g. adolescent pregnancies, sexually-transmitted diseases, and Acquired Immunodeficiency

Syndrome [AIDS]).

5) Ask, "Is it easy or difficult to talk with your son about sex?" If it is difficult, why is it so? Encourage parents who find it relatively easy to talk about sexual issues with their son to share how they accomplish this task with the group.

6) Have the participants consider that if they do not take the initiative in promoting responsible sexual behavior on the part of their son, chances are he will learn about sex "in the street."

7) Provide the participants with the following:
Promoting Responsible Sexual Behavior

- Resolve that your son's basic sex education will take place in your home and not in the street.

- Start to educate your son about sexual issues in early childhood, *e.g., teach correct names for body parts and answer early questions about sex.*

- At the onset of puberty, talk with your son about physical changes taking place with his body. Provide him with facts about normal adolescent events, *e.g., increased interest in opposite sex, wet dreams, masturbation, etc.* Invite your son's questions that will help him separate sexual facts from myths.

- Discuss with your son what his sexuality means with respect to relationships with other people. Discuss with him words such as, *Giving, Caring, Sharing, and Respect*, and what these words mean in the context of a sexual relationship with another person.

- Discuss the nature of fatherhood and the major responsibilities associated with it. Have your son consider that physically he may be able to make a baby, but is he ready to be a father?

- Talk openly with your son about graphic sexual messages and images presented in contemporary CD's, music videos, TV programs, and movies. Help him to evaluate such messages and images and place them into his emerging value system.
- Discuss with your son what his sexuality means in terms of his religious or spiritual values.
- When you feel that your son has reached an appropriate age, conduct frank discussions about issues such as "safe-sex," sexually transmitted diseases, and AIDS.
- If you still find it difficult talking to your son about sex, provide him with well-written books or other resources that explain sexual issues. Additionally, call upon a responsible and trusted adult male relative or friend to discuss sexual issues with your son.

6) Encourage the participants to help each other develop specific proactive strategies for enhancing responsible behavior to incorporate into their personal action plans.

Session 7   *Communicating with your Son*

Goal: To enhance participants' ability to promote unrestrictive communication with their sons about important life issues.

Methods of Facilitation

1) Pose the following to the participants: "If I were to ask your sons the following questions, what do you

suppose their responses would be?" — Do you talk to your parents about problems you have, or private things that are important to you (things you don't talk about with just anybody?) What do you talk about? Do your parents generally have the time to talk with you?

2) Invite the participants to share the challenges they experience in attempting to communicate with their sons.

3) Share the following guidelines with the participants: Guidelines for Talking with Your Son

- Schedule *"quality time"* with your son at least once a week. This is time when you and he can have uninterrupted and informal time to talk about important issues. Also, use this time to engage in recreational or leisure activities with your son.

- Express an interest in things that are important to him, *e.g., sex, drugs, violence, music, TV programs, movies, sports, events at school, peer relationships, etc.* Invite him to discuss his issues or concerns with you. Remember to talk *to* your son, not *at* him. Avoid moralizing or preaching.

- Don't discount his reality or put down his experiences. Listen when he attempts to tell you about his life and experiences. Appreciate that what might seem frivolous or unimportant to you as an adult, is a major life issue from the perspective of a child or teenager.

- Conduct periodic family meetings or roundtables where you invite discussion of your son's concerns about the family or solicit his input on issues related to family

functioning.
- Respect his space. Acknowledge that there may be times he really is not interested in talking or things he does not wish to share with you. Attempts at forcing him to talk will only hamper communication efforts.

4) Encourage the participants to help each other develop specific proactive strategies for enhancing parent-son communication that can be incorporated into personal action plans.

Session 8   *Promoting School Success*

Goal: To enhance participants' ability to promote academic and social success in school by incorporating parental resources into the educational processes more effectively.

Methods of Facilitation

1) Have the participants share their issues and concerns about their sons' school experiences.

2) Facilitate a discussion of the following questions, "What educational goals do you have for your son? "What do you tell your son about school and getting an education?" "Do you help your son with his homework?" "Do you make sure your son does his homework?" "Do you attend school meetings with your son's teachers?"

3) Share the following guidelines with the participants:

Promoting Your Son's School Success at Home
- Adopt the attitude that, regardless of your own level of formal education, you will have a positive impact on your son's success in school.
- Express to your son the academic expectations you have for him. Communicate that you

expect him to perform in school to the best of his ability.

- Establish a climate in the home that fosters academic achievement. For example, an amount of time, appropriate for your son's age, should be set aside Monday through Thursday evening for academic activities. This should be the time when homework is completed. If your son does not have homework on a given evening, this time should be devoted to reading. During this time-period, televisions, radios, and CD players are not in use. In order to enhance this climate and stress the importance of learning in your home, you should engage in some type of learning activity as well. This might include reading a book or magazine.
- Praise your soon for good school work.

4) Promote educational awareness among the participants in the following ways:
- Explain standardized testing, grading, and placement procedures.
- Provide guidance on how to conduct constructive parent-teacher conferences.
- Explain current curriculum innovations.

5) Encourage the participants to make periodic visits to their son's classroom to check on his progress. Stress that they should not wait for calls from teachers or administrators about academic or social difficulties before they visit schools.

6) Encourage participants to help each other develop specific proactive strategies for promoting school success that can be incorporated into personal action plans.

Concluding Activity

Goal: To have participants reinforce the awareness, knowledge, and skills gained during the workshop and commit themselves to implementing strategies to help empower their sons.

Methods of Facilitation

1) Invite the participants to a celebration marking the end of the workshop. Encourage them to bring their sons to this session. Provide refreshments.

2) Have the participants introduce their son to the group. Encourage the parents to state three things about him which gives them a sense of pride.

3) Review *The Seven Principles of Nguzu Saba.* To reinforce the importance of and a commitment to the action plans developed during the workshop, invite participants to share one parenting strategy they plan to implement. Ask them to explain how their strategy fits into these principles.

4) Show the videotape, *"Black, Male and Successful in America,"* described in chapter 5. Conduct an informal discussion of the question, "What part(s) of the video was most helpful to you as a parent?"

5) Encourage participants to maintain contact with each other to provide a parenting support network.

6) As necessary, help participants make contact with appropriate social support and welfare agencies to assist with various aspects of parenting.

7) For an inspirational ending, select one mother to read the poem *"Mother to Son,"* by Langston Hughes. In many respects, this poem represents the essence of African American parenting.

Conclusion

Ms. Jones' poignant question at the beginning of this chapter is echoed by scores of African American women who find themselves raising male children with out the benefit of an adult male partner. While most do an excellent job of being both mother *and* father to their sons, the task is often overwhelming. For scores of African American parents the challenges associated with raising children are often compounded by the harsh realities of racism and its attendant problems. Ms. Jones and her counterparts face innumerable obstacles as they attempt to raise their sons against the backdrop of ever-increasing societal pressure on Black males. Unfortunately, far too many single African American mothers are watching their sons become negative statistics.

Because the empowerment of Black male youth must begin in the home, with parents who can promote the attitudes, behaviors, and values necessary for academic and social success, *"S.O.N.S."* was developed. It provides a supportive atmosphere for African American parents, particularly single mothers like Ms. Jones, to enhance their innate parenting sense with specific skills and techniques which promote the academic, career and personal success of their young sons.

SUGGESTED WORKSHOP RESOURCES

Alvy, K.T. (1987). *Black parenting: Strategies for Training.* Studio City, CA: Irving Publishers, Inc.

"Black Male and Successful in America." Alexandria, Virginia Public Schools.

Comer, J.P., & Poussaint, A.F. (1975). *Black child care.* New York: Simon & Schuster.

Hill, M. (1992). *Training African American parents for success: An Afrocentric parenting guide.* Cleveland, OH: East End Neighborhood House.

Hopson, D.P., & Hopson, D.S. (1990). *Different and wonderful: Raising Black children in a race-conscious society.* New York: Prentice Hall Press.

Hughes, L. (1970). Mother to son. In L. Higes and A. Bontemps (Eds.), *The poetry of the Negro,* 1746 to 1970 (p. 186). Garden City, NY: Doubleday.

Kunjufu, J. (1984). *Developing positive self-image and discipline in Black children.* Chicago, IL: African American Images.

Perkins, U. (1989). *Afrocentric self-inventory and discovery workbook for African American youth.* Chicago, IL: Third World Press.

REFERENCES

Alvy, K. T. (1985, June). *Parenting programs for Black parents.* Paper presented at the Vermont Conference on the Primary Prevention of Psychopathology. Burlington, VT.

Asante, M. K. (1988). *Afrocentricity.* Trenton NJ: Africa World Press, Inc.

Banks, W., & Grambs, J. (1972). *Black self-concept.* New York: McGraw-Hill.

Billingsley, A. (1968). *Black families in white America.* Englewood Cliffs, NJ: Prentice-Hall.

Billingsley, A. (1992). *Climbing Jacob's ladder: The enduring legacy of African American families.* New York: Simon & Schuster.

Clark, R. (1983). *Family life and school achievement.* Chicago: University Press of Chicago.

Comer, J. P. (1986, February). Parent participation in the schools. *Phi Delta Kappan*, pp. 442-46.

Comer, J. P., & Poussaint, A. F. (1975). *Black child care*. New York: Simon & Schuster.

Crawley, B., & Freeman, E. M. (1993). Themes in the life views of older and younger African American males. *Journal of African American Male Studies*, 1, 15-29

Dash, L. (1989). *When children want children: The urban crises of teenage childbearing*. New York: William Morrow and Co.

Edelman, M.W. (1988). An advocacy agenda for Black families and children. In H. P. McAdoo (Ed.), *Black Families* (pp.291-300). Newbury Park, CA: Sage.

Erikson, E. (1950). *Childhood and society*. New York: Norton.

Frazier, E. F. (1939). *The Negro family in the United States*. Chicago: University of Chicago Press.

Genovese, E. D. (1974). *Roll Jordan roll: The world the slaves made*. New York: Random House.

Giannotti, T. J., & Doyle, R. E. (1982). The effectiveness of parental training on learning disabled children and their parents. *Elementary School Guidance and Counseling, 17,* 131-136.

Goins, B. (1993). Report: Parent involvement. *Childhood Education, 69,* 189-91.

Gordon, T. (1975). *Parent effectiveness training*. New York: New American Library.

Gutman, H. (1976). *The Black family in slavery and freedom: 1750-1925*. New York: Random House.

Hale-Benson, J. (1986). *Black children: Their roots, culture and learning styles*. Baltimore, MD: Johns Hopkins Press.

Hammond, J. M., & Schutz, D. S. (1980). A communication workshop that works for high school students and their parents. *School Counselor, 27*, 300-304.

Harrison, D. S., & Alvy, K.T. (1982). *The context of Black parenting*. Studio City, CA: Center for the Improvement of Child Caring.

Hayles, V. R. (1991). African American strengths: A survey of empirical findings. In R. L. Jones (Ed.), *Black psychology. (3rd ed.)* , (pp. 379-400). Berkeley, CA: Cobb & Henry.

Henderson, A. (1987). *The evidence continues to grow: Parent involvement improves student achievement.* Columbia, MD: National Committee for Citizens in Education.

Hill, M. (1992). *Training African American parents for success: An Afrocentric parenting guide.* Cleveland, OH: East End Neighborhood House.

Hill, R. (1972). *The strengths of Black families.* New York: Emerson-Hall.

Hopson, D. P., & Hopson, D. S. (1990). *Different and wonderful: Raising Black children in a race-conscious society.* New York: Prentice Hall Press.

Lamb, J., & Lamb, W. A. (1978). *Parent education and elementary counseling.* New York: Human Sciences Press.

Lewis, A. (1992). *Helping young urban parents educate themselves and their children.* New York: ERIC Clearinghouse on Urban Education.

Martin, E. P., & Martin, J. M. (1980). *The Black extended family.* Chicago: University of Chicago Press.

McAdoo, H. (1981). *Black families.* Newbury Park, CA: Sage.

McQueen, A. B., & Washington, V. (1988). Effect of intervention on the language facility of poor, Black adolescent mothers and their preschool children. Early Child Development and Care, 33, 137-152.

Moynihan, P. (1965). *The Negro family: The case for national action.* Washington, DC: Office of Policy Planning and Research, U.S. Department of Labor.

Nobles, W. (1974). Africanity: Its role in Black families. *The Black Scholar,* June, 10-17.

Noller, P., & Taylor, R. (1989). Parent education and family relations. *Family Relations, 38,* 196-200.

Ogbu, J. (1988). Cultural diversity and human development. In D. T. Slaughter (Ed.), *Black children and poverty: A developmental perspective* San Francisco: Jossey-Bass.

Piaget, J. (1970). *Science of education and the psychology of the child.* New York: Onion Press.

Pinsker, M., & Geoffrey, K. (1981). A comparison of parent effectiveness training and behavior modification parent training. *Family Relations, 30,* 61-68.

Rainwater, L. (1970). *Behind ghetto walls: Black family life in a federal slum.* Chicago: Aldine.

Slaughter, D. T., & Kuehne, V. S. (1988). Improving Black education: Perspectives on parent involvement. *Urban League Review, 11,*59-75.

Staples, R. (1974). The Black family in evolutionary perspective. *The Black Scholar, 5,* 2-9.

Sudarkasa, N. (1980). African and Afro-American family structure: A comparison. *The Black Scholar, 11,* 37-60.

Sudarkasa, N. (1981). Interpreting the African heritage in Afro-American family organization. In H. P. McAdoo (Ed.), *Black families*, (pp. 37-53). Beverly Hills: Sage Publications.

Warnat, W. (1980). *Guide to parent involvement: Parents as adult learners. Overview of parent involvement programs and practices.* Washington, DC: Adult Learning Potential Institute.

Winters, W. G. (1993). *African American mothers and urban schools: The power of participation.* New York: Lexington Books.

CHAPTER 9

"WHITE MEN CAN'T JUMP," BUT CAN THEY BE HELPFUL?

"I am a White man, what role can I play in helping the Black guys at my school?" Do I even have a role?"

A variation of this question is frequently asked at workshops and conferences on Black male issues. It is generally asked by a White male educator concerned about the academic and social plight of the Black males in his school. He usually asks the question because of a genuine commitment to address the challenges confronting the Black males he is attempting to educate.

As the challenges confronting Black male youth receive increasing media attention, there is a growing awareness that much needs to be done to stem the tide of alienation, frustration, underachievement, and violence that often characterize their life-experience. There is a growing realization that the future not only of African Americans, but ultimately all citizens of the country, rests on insuring that Black male youth have an equal opportunity for educational and social advancement. Many sectors of the American public are beginning to understand that the ultimate well-being of the nation is predicated on providing all young people, regardless of their gender or ethnic background, with opportunities to develop abilities that will make them productive members of society.

While the ultimate responsibility for empowering young Black males rests with the African American family, community, and cultural institutions, concerned individuals from other racial or ethnic backgrounds are realizing that they too must play a role in this important process. Significantly, in recent years individuals from other cultural backgrounds have sought ways to act on their concern and make a commitment to Black male empowerment.

The purpose of this chapter is to help individuals from other racial or ethnic backgrounds channel their concern and commitment into empowering young Black males. The chapter focuses on White males and the role that they can play in promoting academic and social success for Black male youth. White men are the focus of this chapter because of their historical position of power and privilege in American society (Gerzon, 1982; Goldberg, 1976; McIntosh, 1988; Pleck & Sawyer, 1974). They are, arguably, in the best position to assist in the Black male empowerment process.

Three Levels of Intervention

If concerned White men are to become actively involved in the empowerment of Black male youth, then they must consider intervention at three levels: *intrapersonal, interpersonal, and systemic.* These three levels comprise a comprehensive approach to directing energy and talents toward promoting the development of young Black males.

Intrapersonal Intervention

Any White male who is committed to the Black male empowerment process must first examine his own attitudes, behaviors, and values. In recent years, much has been written about men, particularly White middle class men, engaging in activities that will allow them to explore their *"maleness"* and its associated thoughts, feelings and behaviors (Bly, 1990; Keen, 1991). Such introspection should be the first step in any intrapersonal intervention initiative.

White men must accept the fact that having been born White *and* male in the United States, it is very possible that they have been the beneficiary of unearned masculine privilege (McIntosh, 1988). Chances are, that from boyhood, they have been subtly socialized by family, school, and society in general, with a masculine sensibility that is comprised of an awareness that authority, control, and power are their birthright. This awareness is the primary means of insuring personal respect, financial security, and success (Goldberg, 1980; McIntosh, 1988; Pleck & Sawyer, 1974).

It is important, therefore, that White men reflect on their childhood and adolescent experiences as a way to understand the possible impact of this privilege on their psychosocial development. Because privilege is generally taken for granted by most White males, it may be necessary to engage in a conscious effort to discern the impact of masculine privilege. The focal question that must be explored is: *"Has being White and male afforded me advantages and opportunities in society, if so, what are they?"*

When a White male realizes and accepts the possibility that he has been afforded unearned privilege, based solely on his race and gender, it is at that point that he should make a conscious decision about its practical value to his life. He could, for example, decide that its sole value lies in insuring him personal advantage in a society that often limits access to social and economic opportunity based on race and gender. However, he might also decide that his privilege affords him the opportunity to direct energy and resources at increasing access to social and economic opportunity.

The former decision can form the basis for a personal

commitment to social action. If this commitment includes assisting in the empowerment of Black male youth, then the second step in the intrapersonal intervention process should be developing a knowledge of, and appreciation for, the Black male experience.

No White male could credibly attempt to assist in the empowerment of Black male youth without a thorough knowledge of past and contemporary Black history, a complete understanding of the psychological and social effects of racism and oppression on Black male development, and a solid comprehension of the African American cultural experience. Such knowledge, understanding, and comprehension might be enhanced, for example, by reading literature about the Black male experience. Novels such as *Native Son* by Richard Wright, *Invisible Man* by Ralph Ellison, and *Manchild in the Promised Land* by Claude Brown, offer dramatic glimpses into the body, mind, and soul of the Black man. These works stand as classics of American literature and should form the basis for understanding the Black male and the historic challenges he has faced in American society. Likewise, the *Autobiography of Malcolm X* explores the systematic destruction and reconstruction of a Black man in America. It is a powerful analysis of the negative impact of racism and oppression on Black male psychosocial development. The book also affirms Black male commitment, spirituality, and self-discipline. This book is required reading if one is to truly appreciate the nature of Black male empowerment.

In addition to the classic works mentioned above, books by contemporary African American male authors should be considered as part of a knowledge-building process. These might include: *A Man's Life: An Autobiography* by Roger Wilkins, which chronicles the challenges of growing up and succeeding as a middle-class Black male in twentieth-century America. *Bloods: An Oral History of the Vietnam War by Black Veterans* by Wallace Terry, which chronicles the trials and triumphs of Black soldiers, who were disproportionately represented in that war; *Makes Me Wanna Holler: A Young Black Man in America* by Nathan McCall, an autobiography by a *Washington Post* reporter that details his early involvement in crime which led to a prison term; *Breaking Barriers: A Memoir*, by Carl T. Rowan, which chronicles his rise from abject poverty to award-winning columnist and commentator; *Days of Grace: A Memoir*, by Arthur Ashe, which is a poignant exploration of the life of the late trail-blazing athlete and social activist; and *Cool Pose* by Richard Majors, which is a scholarly exploration of the dynamics of Black male behavior.

Each of these representative works examines various aspects of the lives and development of the Black male in contemporary society. Together, with the classic American works, they would provide a White male with an excellent view into the reality of the Black male experience in America.

There is, however, a limit to what can be learned about the Black male experience from books. Much more can be learned by actually being among Black males and interacting with them in their cultural environment. Efforts should be made to visit with Black males, of all ages, at family gatherings, religious services or ceremonies, celebrations, or social and fraternal gatherings. Such experiences can help to raise awareness of, and increase knowledge about, the Black male experience.

Intrapersonal intervention, therefore, consists of developing self-awareness and a personal knowledge-base from which to form a commitment to action on behalf of Black male youth. White men who wish to help empower young Black males must first acknowledge their masculine privilege and commit to using it for social action. Next, they must develop a true appreciation for the Black male experience that comes from an active process of seeking knowledge about it. This awareness- and knowledge-building process, which forms the basis of intrapersonal intervention, must serve as a necessary prelude to intervention at the interpersonal level.

Interpersonal Intervention

The essence of interpersonal intervention for White men seeking to assist with the empowerment of Black male youth, is to find ways to touch the lives of these young people in a systematic fashion. In the educational setting, for example, it may be important for White male teachers, counselors, and administrators to reach out to Black male students and provide them with support and encouragement. This may be particularly important when these students experience negative attitudes or lowered expectations from White educators. Finding time in a busy school day to talk one-on-one with a Black male student about his school experiences or life in general, is a significant way to show concern and it could prove to be an important way to promote the yearning for academic and social success.

Another intervention idea is to assist in developing and implementing empowerment programs such as those described in chapters 4 and 5. While those programs are designed to be facilitated by Black men, White men can actively explore appropriate ways that they may be effective in supportive roles with such empowerment initiatives. For example, they might offer their services as resource persons who can speak on various issues or topics covered in the programs. While they can not teach Black boys how to become Black men, White men should still find ways to share their wisdom about, and unique vision of, manhood.

A final suggestion is to participate in a big brother-type program. Such programs exist under a variety of names in communities throughout the country. In many instances, these programs are constantly looking for men, regardless of ethnic background, who are willing to make a time commitment to Black male youth. A "big brother" participates in a variety of recreational or educational activities, usually on a weekly basis, with a boy who is paired with him. As a "big brother," a White man would have the opportunity to spend time with a young Black male and serve as an important role model or mentor.

Interpersonal intervention implies getting up close and personal with Black male youth, either individually or in groups.

With systematic interpersonal interventions, White men can become important allies to those in Black communities who are dedicated to promoting academic and social success among Black male youth. As an ally, White men can also initiate important changes for Black males at the systems level as well.

Systemic Intervention

Systemic intervention is the process of impacting upon an environment in order to bring about systems-level change. Such change will ultimately benefit those individuals within that environment or system. Many of the challenges facing young Black males are the result of their reaction to alienating and oppressive forces within their environment. Therefore, full empowerment for Black male youth can only take place when systemic impediments to their development can be removed

For White males, this third level of intervention may ultimately be the most important. Given their traditional societal privilege, they are, in the best position to influence systemic change for the benefit of Black male youth. For example, White men in positions of power in educational and related social settings should use their influence to mandate an institutional commitment to promote the academic, career, and personal-social development of young Black males. Part of this commitment might include endorsing the development of empowerment programs, such as those described in chapters 4, 5, 6, 7, and 8, and working to remove institutional barriers to their implementation.

Another important example of systemic intervention would involve White males working to raise the level of awareness within their own communities about the issues and challenges facing Black male youth. It is important, for example, to find forums through which myths and stereotypes about Black males can be dispelled. Such forums could also mobilize resources in the White community for social action that would benefit not only Black-male youth, but all young people.

A further community-level intervention involves political action. White males can advocate for a national and local political agenda that mandates improving the quality of life for all children and adolescents. Such an agenda should hold political leadership accountable for promoting legislation that will promote Black-male empowerment in crucial areas such as health, education, and crime prevention.

Finally, White men should consider developing empowerment-type programs for young White males. Significantly, while major differences exist, White-male youth face many of the same challenges encountered by their Black-male counterparts as they attempt to master the developmental tasks of childhood and adolescence. Developed and implemented in a manner comparable to programs for Black-male youth, the goals of White-male empowerment initiatives should include: developing skills for academic success, promoting positive and responsible behavior, and fostering positive masculine identities. A major focus of such programs should be to help young White males develop attitudes of tolerance and respect for cultural and gender diversity. Such attitudes will, in a small way, help to insure a future environment that is characterized by mutual respect and understanding.

Conclusion

"White Men Can't Jump," the title of a recent motion picture, explores the unlikely friendship that develops between two amateur basketball players, one Black the other White, who use the game to hustle unsuspecting opponents. In a lighthearted fashion, the movie examines many myths and stereotypes about abilities that are presumed to be race-and

gender-specific, such as jumping ability in basketball. The movie suggests that once individuals get beyond such biased notions, true friendship and beneficial working alliances can be forged between Black and White men.

Given the magnitude of the challenges that often confront young Black males in contemporary society, working alliances between a variety of committed individuals is needed. White men are uniquely qualified to be partners in such alliances. If they are committed, they have an important role to play. While they may not have the same credibility that Black men may possess in the empowerment process, White men's historical advantages in American society often places resources at their disposal that can affect change at both the individual and systems level.

White males can only mobilize such resources, however, after developing self-awareness and a knowledge base to guide their commitment. They must understand their own attitudes, values, and behaviors, as well as appreciate the Black male experience, in order to be effective and credible partners for Black male empowerment.

If a generation of Black male youth is allowed to be lost, it will effect the well-being of not only African American people, but the entire nation as well. White men concerned about the future of the country and its youth, must commit themselves to playing a role, no matter how small, in the empowerment of young Black males.

Suggested Resources on the Black Male Experience

Ashe, A., & Ampersand, A. (1993). *Days of grace: A memoir.* New York: Alfred A. Knopf.

Brown, C. (1965). *Manchild in the promised land.* New York: Macmillan.

Ellison, R. (1952). *Invisible man.* New York: Random House.

Haley, A., & X, M. (1964) *The autobiography of Malcolm X.* New York: Grove Press.

Majors, R., & Billson, J. M. (1993). *Cool pose: The dilemmas of black manhood in America.* New York: Simon and Schuster.

McCall, N. (1994). *Makes me wanna holler: A young Black man in America.* New York: Random House.

Rowan, C.T. (1991). *Breaking the barriers: A memoir.* Boston: Little, Brown and Co.

Terry, W. (1984). *Bloods: An oral history of the Viet Nam War by Black veterans.* New York: Random House.

Wilkins, R. (1982). *A man's life: An autobiography.* New York: Simon and Schuster.

Wright, R. (1940). *Native son.* New York: Harper and Brothers.

References

Bly, R. (1990). *Iron John: A book about men.* Reading, MA: Addison-Wesley.

Gerzon, M. (1982). *A choice of heroes: The changing face of American manhood.* Boston: Houghton Mifflin.

Goldberg, H. (1980). *The new male: From self-destruction to self-care.* New York: New American Library.

Keen, S. (1991). *Fire in the belly: On being a man.* New York: Bantam Books.

McIntosh, P. (1988). *White privilege and male privilege: A personal account of coming to see correspondences through work in women's studies.* Working paper No. 189. Wellesley, MA: Wellesley College Center for Research on Women.

Pleck, J. H. & Sawyer, J. (Eds.) (1974). *Men and masculinity.* Englewood Cliffs, NJ: Prentice-Hall.

CHAPTER 10

"The Malcolm X Principle": Self-Help for Young Black Males

Malcolm X has become a major figure in the history of the twentieth century. During much of his adult life he was both feared and revered for his rhetoric and actions. His life and work stand as a testament to African American struggle and triumph. His autobiography (1964), which chronicles his life and work, is an American classic. It is also a source of inspiration for every African American. Significantly, the book also provides an important blueprint for Black male empowerment.

Malcolm's autobiography details his early life and the racist oppression that eventually forced him into a life of crime. Because of his criminal activity, he was sentenced to prison and served a seven-year term. However, it was while he was in prison that Malcolm's life took a dramatic turn. Through the force of his own will, he was able to turn his life around and make a positive commitment to the struggle of Black people and to himself as a Black man. While in prison he was exposed to the teachings of Elijah Muhammad, the leader of the Nation of Islam, or the "Black Muslims." Elijah Muhammad's teachings inspired Malcolm to engage in a self-improvement process. He initiated a program designed to strengthen his body, mind, and spirit.

There were four important dimensions to Malcolm's push for self-improvement. The first of these was a belief in a higher power. Malcolm came to accept the Islamic concept of God (Allah). This acceptance gave him spiritual direction and provided him a new moral center to his life.

The second dimension of Malcolm's self-improvement was a sense of interconnectedness. He joined the Nation of Islam and became a Muslim. This put him in touch with a group of people who were proud of their African cultural heritage and who were dedicated to a way of life bound by a set of religious principles. It also forged a link for Malcolm with Black history and culture, which provided him with a therapeutic knowledge of himself as a man of African descent.

The third important dimension for Malcolm was the development of a reverence and respect for knowledge. Malcolm cultivated a curiosity about the world of ideas and dedicated himself to obtaining true knowledge. While in prison, he read voraciously and became acquainted with important historical and philosophical ideas. Through his reading he also discovered the truth about the richness and significance of Black culture. In an attempt to improve his knowledge of words, he even copied an entire dictionary by hand.

Malcolm's final motivator was self-discipline. He committed himself to improving his body, mind, and soul, and developed the inner strength to accomplish this. He imposed upon himself physical, mental, and emotional rigor that allowed him to survive prison life and, ultimately, channel energy into improving himself.

As a result of his own efforts, Malcolm left prison transformed. He had become aware of the power dynamics in his life and had developed the skills and capacity for gaining control over his life. He began to exercise these skills and capacity for the uplifting of Black people. In other words, Malcolm had become empowered (McWhirter, 1994). No longer a criminal, Malcolm had become a visionary leader who dedicate the rest of his life to the empowerment of Black people.

The self-help strategy that Malcolm X employed in prison serves as a model for young Black males who often find themselves locked into cycles of poverty, violence, unemployment, or substance abuse. The dimensions of his strategy comprise what can be called *"The Malcom X Principle."* This principle rests on the notion that, ultimately, the only person who can empower a Black male youth, is himself.

The Malcolm X Principle evolves from the following concepts: a belief in a higher power, a sense of belonging or kinship, a reverence and respect for knowledge, and self-discipline. Taken together, these concepts form the basis of a self-help philosophy for all young Black males. The empowerment initiatives discussed in the other chapters in this book should attempt to instill these basic principles in Black male youth.

Belief in a Higher Power

A cornerstone of self-help must be a belief in a higher power. A Black male youth must develop a believe in a force or forces greater than himself. There have never been a group of people at any time in history that did not have a spiritual belief in such forces. Such a belief gives meaning and ultimate purpose to life.

The focal point of a Black male's attitudes, behaviors, and values must be his sense of spirituality. His belief in his own sense of empowerment must start with his belief in powers or natural forces greater than himself.

Sense of Belonging or Kinship

If a young Black male is to have both a sense of his own empowerment and the ability to act to help himself, then he must feel a sense of belonging to a group. Self-help cannot take place if one is experiencing a sense of alienation. A Black male youth must internalize the essence of the traditional African cultural ethos, *"I am because we are, and because we are, therefore I am."* He must feel interconnected with individuals with life-affirming attitudes and values who can provide him with validation and support.

Reverence and Respect for Knowledge

A Black male youth must continually engage in the process

of acquiring knowledge. He must appreciate that ignorance oppresses, and that knowledge liberates. Developing a reverence and respect for knowledge should motivate him to open his mind to a wide range of ideas and concepts. He must come to realize that true knowledge will nourish his body and soul as well as his mind.

Self-Discipline

If a Black male youth is to empower himself, then he must develop an internal locus of control and responsibility. In far too many cases, a young Black male has order and control imposed him from external sources. He should commit, therefore, to imposing order and control over his own life. For example, learning to delay gratification, eating in a healthy fashion, or resisting peer pressure, would be important aspects in fostering self-discipline.

Empowering Oneself Through Networking on the Internet

Access to quality information is a key component of empowerment. Leaning what others have done in a given situation with what results can be immensely helpful to someone in making decisions and plans. Also, joining a network of individuals who share common concerns and interests, such as a support group in dealing with test anxiety or avoiding chemical abuse, can be a powerful resource for an individual. The advent of the Internet and the ability to surf the net to identify the wide range of resources and listservs (on-line interactive groups) which a person can access/join can be extremely valuable. Preparing young persons of all ages, races and ethnic identities to use new forms of electronic information gathering and networking on the Internet can be an enormous "head start" for them. It thus is important that all young persons learn how to use and participate in the new electronic communication. ERIC/CASS, through its many user services, can assist persons to gain access to and use the different resources.

Conclusion

Ultimately, the empowerment of young Black males rests within themselves. They must find the inner resources to promote their own educational and social success. While empowerment programs such as those described in this book are important, they can only serve to instill the notion of a personal commitment in participants. Each young man must then decide for himself whether to act on that commitment. He must decide whether he has the personal resources to help himself. Malcolm X stands a powerful example of a young Black male who through his own commitment found such resources. His method for doing so provides a self-help blueprint. *The Malcolm X Principle*, therefore, is the key to empowerment. Today, as Black male youth don popular hats and T-shirts with the image of Malcom X emblazoned on them, they should pause to reflect what that image really represents. It is the image of Black man who through the sheer force of his own will and commitment overcame great odds and negative circumstances. Surely they can do the same.

References

Haley, A., & X, M. (1964). *The autobiography of Malcolm X*. New York: Grove Press.

McWhirter, E. H. (1994). *Counseling for Empowerment*. Alexandria, VA: ACA

CHAPTER 11

A COUNSELOR CALL TO ACTION: A COMPREHENSIVE APPROACH TO EMPOWERING YOUNG BLACK MALES

The distressing statistics related to the lack of basic competencies, disruptive behavior, and dropout rates for Black male students in America's schools present a major challenge to professional counselors and other educators. Definitive and comprehensive strategies must be employed to address this challenge. As the preceding chapters have suggested, new perspectives on ways to promote the empowerment of young Black males are needed. Professional counselors, along with educators, parents, and other concerned individuals, are all major influences in offering solutions to the educational and social challenges confronting this often embattled group of young people. A concerted effort is needed to develop comprehensive empowerment strategies that reflect the needs and realities of young Black males. Professional counselors can be in the forefront of coordinating such strategies. Implicit in such strategies must be the notion that counselors are agents of change; they possess the knowledge and skill to translate caring into empowerment initiatives. As this book has suggested, such initiatives must include programmed interventions that embrace the Black male in his home, school, and community.

This final chapter reviews specific counselor roles and functions considered critical for empowering Black male youth.

In addition, important counselor functions related to the concerns of school personnel and the educational commitment of the African American community, and members of other racial groups, are presented. These roles and functions form the basis for a comprehensive school-based Black male empowerment initiative.

The Counselor and the Black Male Student

The achievements, aspirations, and pride of many Black males have been seriously stifled in the school setting. Concerned counselors must help empower young Black males so as to develop in them the attitudes, behaviors, and skills for success in school and the demanding world beyond. Counselors, therefore, must assume the role of student-development facilitator and engage in functions that transcend the traditional boundaries of educational helping. Specific empowerment strategies are needed for heightening awareness, expanding skills, and maximizing options on the part of Black male youth.

Personal-Social Empowerment

Instilling a positive self-identity in young Black males is a primary empowerment function for student-development facilitators. Such a task is underscored by the identity of failure fostered in scores of Black males by educational experiences that are often insensitive to the dynamics of their psychosocial development or their cultural realities. A positive self-identity must serve as the basis for all goals; for it is only when Black males accept themselves and their realities with a sense of pride that tangible educational gains are possible. The interventions described in chapters 4 and 5, for example, represent empowerment models whose fundamental goal is to promote positive self-identity among participants.

Academic Empowerment

Counselors and teachers must collaborate to foster the development of motivation and skills for academic achievement among Black male students. Concerned counselors need to work with teachers to insure that the teaching-learning process maximizes the potential of Black male youth. This might entail consulting with teachers to provide such things as tutorial programs, academic-planning initiatives, or study-skills seminars. In addition, counselors should adopt an active role in any school-system initiatives which might include the implementation of controversial educational programs, such as recent efforts to form separate classes or schools for Black males.

Career Development

The world of work for many Black males has been landscaped with unfulfilled dreams, wasted potential, dashed hopes, and economic struggle. Given this history, the issue of career interest and choice becomes a complex dimension in the development of Black male youth. The committed counselor, therefore, must consider the social pressures on Black male career development and restructure traditional career guidance accordingly. Career empowerment for Black male students should include disseminating information on, and encouraging the exploration of, nonstereotyped jobs and careers. Importantly, career-development interventions should provide adult Black males as career role models and mentors who can explain their perceptions and experiences in the world of work.

The Counselor and the Educational System

In working with the educational system to empower young Black males, counselors must assume the role of educational advocate. Such professionals understand that educational problems do not always start with Black male students, but often exist in the system. Educational advocacy begins with a knowledge of systemic barriers to quality education for Black male youth and calls for the development of skills to effectively challenge these barriers.

Educational advocates consult with teachers, administrators, and related professionals to identify alienating factors in attitudes, behaviors, or policies concerning Black male students. They also actively participate with educators on ways to incorporate the Black male cultural experience into the total curriculum. The curriculum guide presented in chapter 7 is an example of such educational advocacy.

The Counselor and the Black Community

The Black male brings to school cultural attitudes, behaviors, and values fostered in the institutions within his community. However, cultural insensitivity in the educational system often invalidates the cultural realities of these Black institutions. Because of this, valid representatives of these institutions are often excluded from serious consideration in the educational empowerment of Black males.

Counselors can play an active role in bridging this gap by serving as a liaison between the school and the Black community. They can work to promote the development and incorporation of family and community resources into the educational empowerment process for Black male youth. The program for enhancing the parenting skills of African American parents described in chapter 8 is typical of such an effort. Other counselor efforts might also include coordinating paraprofessional development programs, such as the one described in chapter 6, to involve responsible, committed, and mature Black men from the community in empowerment interventions for male youth.

The Counselor and Concerned Individuals from other Racial Backgrounds

The Black male may interact with individuals from a variety of racial backgrounds in the educational setting. Many of these individuals have a limited understanding of, or negative preconceived notions about Black male youth that often interfere with academic progress. However, scores of individuals have a true commitment to insuring the opportunities of Black male youth.

Counselors can help these individuals develop the personal awareness and knowledge so they can assist African American parents and community members in fostering Black male success. The ideas discussed in chapter 9, for example, provide a framework for channeling the commitment and resources of men from other racial groups into the Black male empowerment process.

The Challenge

The future status of Black men in America depends, in large measure, on the ability of educators to improve the academic success of Black male youth. Counselors can play a proactive role in empowering Black males for maximum educational achievement and productive lives. Accomplishing this, however, will require a comprehensive and systematic approach to the issues of educational empowerment. Such an approach implies a rejection of many long-standing traditions characteristic of school counseling. In assuming the roles and attempting to implement the functions considered in this chapter, counselors can no longer commit themselves solely to the task of facilitating Black male adjustment to the educational system. Empowerment for Black male students will be enhanced by planning strategically, by including support from school personnel, by revising curriculums to reflect Black male realities, and by enlisting the cultural expertise of representatives from the Black community. These things should be done with the aim of having Black males persist and succeed in the educational system.

There is an old African saying, *"It takes an entire village to raise a child."* If a Black male child in the United States is to grow into a strong, competent, and productive man, then a communal effort is needed to insure that this happens. The community involved in this effort should include parents, educators, and all those who have a commitment to the future well-being of young people. Counseling professionals who understand the crisis and the challenges associated with being Black and male in America constitute a potent force for making educational and social empowerment for Black male youth a reality. They can marshal the collective community resources necessary to promote the development of young Black males. They stand ready to answer the call to action. The "Ronalds" and "Maliks," as well as the other present and future *"native sons"* are waiting for such action. They deserve no less.

APPENDIX A
Four Poems

I, Too

I, too, sing America.

I am the darker brother.
They send me to eat in the kitchen
When company comes,
But I laugh,
And eat well,
And grow strong.

Tomorrow,
I'll be at the table
When company comes.
Nobody'll dare
Say to me,
"Eat in the kitchen,"
Then.

Besides,
They'll see how beautiful I am
And be ashamed—

I, too, am America.

—By Langston Hughes

Reprinted with permission of Alfred A. Knopf, New York.

The Negro Speaks of Rivers

(To W.E.B. DuBois)

I've known rivers:
I've known rivers ancient as the world and older than the
flow of human blood in human veins.
My soul has grown deep like the rivers.

I bathed in the Euphrates when dawns were young.
I've built my hut near the Congo and it lulled me to sleep.
I looked upon the Nile and raised the pyramids above it.
I heard the singing of the Mississippi when Abe Lincoln
went down to New Orleans, and I've seen its muddy
bosom turn all golden in the sunset.

I've known rivers:
Ancient, dusky rivers.

My soul has grown deep like the rivers.

—by Langston Hughes

Mother to Son

Well, son, I'll tell you:
Life for me ain't been no crystal stair.
It's had tacks in it,
And splinters,
And boards torn up,
And places with no carpet on the floor—
Bare.
But all the time
I'se been a-climbin' on,
And reachin' landin's,
And turning corners,
And sometimes goin' in the dark
Where there ain't been no light.
So boy, don't you turn back.
Don't you set down on the steps
"Cause you finds it's kinder hard.
Don't you fall now—
For I'se still goin', honey,
I'se still climbin',
And life for me ain't been no crystal stair.

—By Langston Hughes

Reprinted with permission of Alfred A. Knopf, New York

To a Negro Boy Graduating

Be wary, lad; the road up which you go
Is long and steeper than you dare to think.
And since you leave in darkness, lad, be slow—
Test every spring before you bend to drink;
Learn now the rose may hide a hundred scars,
The welcome breeze may herald storms ahead,
And though your eyes would trace the course of stars
Or gaze on gray horizons growing red,
Let caution rule your step that you may see
The gaping pit, the waiting bog, the wall
of white which you must scale. Go carefully
And hopefully; but if somewhere you sink or fall,
Remember where you walked you smoothed the way
That those who follow may discover day.

—By Eugene T. Maleska

Reprinted with permission of Doubleday, New York

APPENDIX B
Three Pride Activities

What is Pride? (Grades 6-8)

Purpose: To help develop self-concept

Materials: Pencil and paper.

Introduction: Write the meaning for the word "pride" on the board. Have someone read the meaning aloud. Ask the question, "How many of you have pride?" Have the students make a list of things in which they have pride.

Variation: Younger children could draw pictures of things in which they have pride. Older children could discuss how and why men have fought for pride of self and country.

Correlation: This activity could be integrated with language arts activities, emphasizing correct spelling and writing skills.

King's Crown (Grades K-4)

Purpose: To increase student's awareness of African History.

Materials: Construction paper, stapler, pencil, scissors, and a ruler.

Introduction: Africa had many great kings and queens. Probably one of the most outstanding kings was the Ashanti king. One queen who will always be remembered is Cleopatra, the beautiful queen of Egypt. Many of the kings and queens wore beautiful crowns to symbolize their rank. The crowns we are going to make will not be made of diamonds or gold like the African crowns, but ours will have a close resemblance.

Directions: Cut regular size construction paper into halves. Have the children draw an outline of the top of the crown. Cut out the pattern. Staple the two ends together to fit the student's head.

Variation: The teacher could bring in a short report on famous African kings or queens. She could bring in pictures from encylopedias and resource books related to this subject.

On Being Black (Grades 1-4)

Purpose: To make students aware of occupations that many Black people have,

Materials: Paper, pencils.

Introduction: Today we are going to talk about what it means to be Black in the various occupational fields. There is a list of questions on the board for you to copy.

Questions: (Listed on the board)

	Yes	No
1. Do you know a Black baseball player?	☐	☐
2. Do you know a Black doctor?	☐	☐
3. Do you know a Black Lawyer?	☐	☐
4. Do you know a Black carpenter?	☐	☐
5. Do you know a Black actor?	☐	☐
6. Do you know a Black dentist?	☐	☐

Instructions: Put a check in either the Yes or No box for each question. After the children have finished checking each question, discuss the following: How many people know a Black doctor, lawyer, etc.? Total the number of people who know someone in each category. How many people would like to be

working in one of these occupations and
why? Do you think that color makes a difference in
some of these occupations? Why?

Variation: Children might enjoy doing research to
discover unusual professions in which Black people
are involved and report back to the class.

Correlation: A lesson in the use of resource materials (how to
locate specific types of information) would be useful
for this activity.

These three activities are from a book called *Pride: A Handbook of Black Studies Techniques for the Classroom Teacher* by Clifford D. Watson. The book at present is out of print. It was published in 1971 by Educational Services, Inc. in Stevensville, Michigan.